TIM LEWIS

The
DOMINO
Effect

TIM LEWIS

The
DOMINO
Effect

Changing Your Life
One Decision at a Time

GOSPEL
ADVOCATE
A TRUSTED NAME SINCE 1855

Published by Gospel Advocate Co.
1006 Elm Hill Pike, Nashville, TN 37210
www.gospeladvocate.com

ISBN: 978-0-89225-661-7

DEDICATION

To my wife, Tawni Day Lewis.
Marrying her was one of my best decisions.

And to my children, Macy, Callie and Ryder,
in the hope that they will make the kinds of
decisions described in these pages.

Table of
CONTENTS

FOREWORD

An abundant life depends on our making good decisions from early in life until the very end. Just as a skyscraper reaches the heavens one brick at a time, a human being reaches the peak of happiness and service by making good choices day after day.

Tim Lewis is a believer in the power of good life choices, and he has given us a book to prove it. More than a book, his own life has shown that people can and should make good decisions and that decisions, whether good or bad, have far-reaching consequences. Because a meaningful life depends on good choices, *The Domino Effect* is a book needed by both young and old.

Tim grew up in Pennsylvania. As a boy, he made the decision to follow Jesus. That was the most important decision he ever made, and that decision has led to other wise decisions that have shaped his life and ministry. His decision to be a disciple of Jesus Christ influenced his decision to attend Oklahoma Christian University in Oklahoma City, Okla. As an English major, he honed his speaking and writing skills for what appeared at the time to be a life's work in the classroom.

One of his faculty heroes, however, was Avon Malone, a motivational teacher and preacher, who had the God-given ability to inspire young men to preach the gospel. An avid basketball enthusiast himself, Avon enjoyed a good relationship with Tim Lewis, the student athlete, who played on Oklahoma Christian's basketball team. As Avon visited with Tim about his future, he sensed that the Lord was leading Tim to go into full-time ministry. With great love and a growing passion for serving Jesus Christ, Tim soon made the decision to enter the ministry of the Word and dedicate himself totally to that work. So far as I know, he has never wavered from that good decision.

When an opportunity came Tim's way to attend graduate school for ministerial studies, he said "yes" and threw himself into his work. I had the privilege of being one of his professors. When he had the opportunity to do a summer internship with Robert K. Oglesby Sr., well-known author and minister of the Waterview Church of Christ in Richardson, Texas, he jumped at the possibility. When the invitation came to preach for a loving local church in Mount Vernon, Mo., his answer was "yes." When the door opened for him to work with the dynamic North MacArthur Church of Christ in Oklahoma City, he wasted no time in accepting the opportunity. In the very best sense of the word, Tim is a "yes" man and a "can do" kind of person. His life trajectory in ministry has been based on making good choices for the Lord and encouraging others to do the same.

As his ministry has grown, Tim Lewis has become a leader beyond the borders of his local congregation. Besides being a frequent speaker at area-wide gatherings and a coordinator of the popular Oklahoma lectureship, "Affirming the Faith," he has been a positive force in the movement to restore today's church to what God wanted it to be from the very beginning. Readers will always see and hear an appeal to biblical authority in Tim's preaching and in *The Domino Effect*.

Dr. Howard W. Norton,
Searcy, Ark.

ACKNOWLEDGMENTS

To borrow from the inspired language of Romans 1:14, "I am a debtor." First and foremost I am indebted to my parents, David and Linda Lewis. The difficult decision they made to reform their lives at such a crucial time made faith and salvation a reality for me. I also feel a strong debt of gratitude to Neil Anderson for befriending me and believing that I had it in me to write a book, to Greg Tidwell for his constant support and encouragement and to Dennis Loyd, my editor and new friend. I would never have completed this book without his patience and skillful guidance. I am also indebted to Howard Norton for writing the foreword.

I am indebted to the church of Jesus Christ. I love the Lord's church and feel indebted to all of the congregations that taught, converted, nurtured and trained me. I want to thank the Mount Vernon congregation for giving me my first work in ministry. Many of the ideas in this book were first presented to the young people who were there during those joyful years when I worked as both the preacher and youth minister. I also want to thank the North MacArthur Church of Christ for listening to the sermon series that I presented as I developed each chapter of this book. After 11 years of working with these incredible Christians this is still my dream job.

Finally, I would not feel right if I didn't mention the people who read the earliest drafts of this book and always gave me positive feedback and helpful suggestions for making each chapter better; among others I am thankful for Claudia Crain, Kristin Lee, Mike Lewis, Jeremy Roberts and Cory Slaughter.

I am the beneficiary of countless preachers, professors and writers whose sermons, classes and books have blessed my life and faith. I have done my best to credit those whose thoughts I have borrowed, but in some cases I have absorbed what I have learned from others into my own thoughts and have repeated the information so often that it has become part of me. The original source has been forgotten but this book would not have been possible without the contribution that many others have made to my understanding of the Christian faith.

INTRODUCTION

The domino effect – the imagery connected to that term is memorable. As a child, I never played dominos, but I certainly played with them. I set them up in elaborate designs and then tipped the first one and watched the chain reaction as each domino fell and toppled the one next to it. But what does any of this have to do with the life-changing decisions described in this book? More than what you might imagine. The first domino is crucial. Everything starts with the Word of God.

The person who decides to base every decision on the Bible will inevitably glorify God. The one who seeks to glorify God will ultimately imitate Jesus. The one who imitates Jesus will always seek first God's kingdom. When the kingdom comes first in a person's life, that person will live by the Golden Rule and saturate his life with prayer. When a person does all of the things just mentioned, his life will become incredibly influential and if he hopes to maintain that influence, he will diligently purify his thoughts. A pure mind that is not contaminated or distracted by evil is free to focus on eternal things like the promise of a home with God. The progression is undeniable. Each good decision leads to the next; it is a domino effect.

Bear in mind, however, that the process just described also works in reverse. People who refuse to make Bible-based decisions will not glorify God, they will not imitate Jesus, and they will not seek first the kingdom. People who have little or no regard for the kingdom will not bother to pray, follow the Golden Rule, guard their influence, purify their thoughts or spend much time thinking about eternal things. Each bad decision leads to the next. It is a negative version of the domino effect – a chain reaction that leads from bad to worse.

We all have a potential self – the person we could have been or the one we might yet become – so much depends on the decisions we make. There is, within each person, the potential for remarkable goodness. There is also the potential for incredible evil. We are not fated or predestined to be one or the other. God has blessed us with the freedom of choice. If the premise of this book is correct and you really are writing your life story one day and one decision at a time, then you have the power to determine how your story ends. Everything hinges on tipping the first domino. Make sure it falls in the right direction.

Chapter 1

Decisions Make a Difference

Why Are They So Important?

Decisions. You make hundreds of them every single day. You will make hundreds of thousands of them in your lifetime. Some will be much easier to make than others. Not every decision is life-altering; but some are. In fact some decisions are so important they not only alter the course of your life but they also dramatically impact your relationship with God. Robert Frost wrote, "Two roads diverged in a wood, and I – I took the one less traveled by, and that has made all the difference." When you come to a fork in the path of life, the decision you make and the course you choose to follow will not only affect your personal life and faith but it may also change the direction of someone else's life as well.

My father is what you might describe as a modern-day prodigal. His return to the Father's house gave birth to my faith. Dad dropped out of high school the summer after his junior year. He enlisted in the Air Force and was stationed in Roswell, N.M. While he was there, he met a member of the Main Street Church of Christ who taught him the gospel and baptized him for the remission of his sins.

Just six months after his conversion, he moved back home to Pennsylvania and gradually fell away from the church. After 20 years in the "far country" of sin, he took me, my mom and my two brothers to vacation Bible school at the Fourth and Arch Street Church of Christ in Sunbury, Pa. We went to Bible class every night that week. We thought my dad had lost his mind because we were not "church-going" people.

My dad was a drinking man. He hosted beer-drinking parties in our home. I do not have any Bible school memories from my early childhood, but I do remember those parties. I remember how much fun it was to have all those interesting characters in our home. I also remember how lonely I felt when the party was over, and we were left in our empty house with our empty lives and our guilty consciences. I had seen and heard a lot of things in my young life, but nobody had ever told me the story of God's redeeming love. My father knew that story, but he never made any effort to share it with me or any of the rest of my family until that one week of VBS. That was the beginning of a whole new life for us.

Alcohol slowly disappeared from our home. Many of my father's rowdy friends must have figured out they could no longer find what they were looking for at our house. One by one they all disappeared; even some of our relatives were no longer as comfortable around us as they once were. We started going to church on Sunday morning, Sunday evening and Wednesday night. Eventually my dad was restored. My mother, my two brothers and I were all baptized. In time, with great patience and careful instruction, my family grew in faith and practice. My dad served as an elder. My mother has taught children's Bible classes for more than 30 years and is still active in her service. My brother Jeff serves as a deacon. My brother Mike and I are both gospel preachers.

It took remarkable courage for my dad to change his life the way he did. I have often wondered how different my life would be right now if he had not made the decision to repent and be restored. That one decision changed the course of my life. It was a defining moment, a turning point. So many of the good things I have experienced might never have happened without that one influential decision. His return to Christ was like the tipping of the first domino. It set off a chain reaction of countless blessings. If I have learned anything from my father's example, it is that decisions are extremely important. Just one key decision can radically change the direction of a man's life.

Decisions Affect Character

Decisions are important because they affect your character. The decisions you make today determine the person you will become tomorrow. In a sense you are writing your life story one day, and one decision, at a time. Your character and personality are the direct result and the sum total of every decision you have ever made. In other words, whoever you are right now is exactly who you have decided to be.

Some will resent that implication. Others, I am certain, will protest that such a statement is judgmental and unfair. An appeal might be made to the irresistible forces of nature and nurture. Some will claim they cannot help who they have become because they were genetically predisposed to be that way or because their environment made it impossible for them to be anything else.

This mindset not only removes all personal accountability but it also makes every one of us a victim of circumstance. Yet we see examples all the time of people who have overcome the odds by coming out of an almost impossible situation and accomplishing something meaningful with their lives. Take for example the two sons of an alcoholic. One grows up to follow in his father's footsteps, and the other does not. When asked how such a thing is even possible, both point to their father. One sees his father as an excuse and claims, "I drink because my father did." The other sees his father as his greatest motivation saying, "I was determined never to take a single drink," and then explains, "I didn't want to become like my father."

Judas is a biblical example of how decisions affect character. He had so many advantages. Jesus selected him to serve as one of the 12 apostles. He had intimate access to Jesus for the duration of His earthly ministry. Think about that. Judas had a front row seat to the ministry of Christ; more than that, he had a backstage pass. He heard the sermons, saw the miracles and enjoyed private access to Jesus, a privilege many were not afforded. And despite all of those undeserved advantages, he sold the Savior for 30 pieces of silver. How could such a thought enter his heart? It seems unthinkable if you look at it as an isolated event; but in reality, it was not an isolated event. It was the culmination of a series of character-forming decisions.

John tells us that Judas was a thief. He had charge of the money box, and "he used to take what was put in it" (John 12:6). According to Matthew, Judas "went to the chief priests and said, 'What are you willing to give me if I deliver Him to you?'" (Matthew 26:14-15). The chief priests didn't come to Judas; he went to them. The idea of paying someone to betray Jesus was not their idea; it was his. That small detail is subtle but significant. This tragic and concluding chapter of Judas' life did not destroy his character; it revealed his character. A lifetime of previous decisions had warped his personality, which is what made it possible for him to betray his friend and teacher for personal gain.

You must be careful not to allow the same kind of thing to happen to you. The decisions you make each day are leaving an indelible imprint on your character. You are either growing closer to God in your character or drifting further and further from Him.

When the late Bishop Taylor Smith was a young man, he took as his motto four simple words: "As now – So then." This is an important concept, and the sooner you learn and apply it the better chance you will have of making meaningful and lasting changes to your character and personality. Far too many Christians are under the mistaken impression that they can be one thing now but then somehow, almost magically, grow to become something entirely different and significantly better in the future.

I want to warn you that it is not easy to change your personality or to improve your character. You can't wake up one morning, flip a switch and suddenly become a different person. Many have tried this and discovered that sinful habits are much easier to form than they are to break. Jeremiah wisely asked, "Can the Ethiopian change his skin or the leopard its spots? Then may you also do good who are accustomed to do evil" (Jeremiah 13:23 NKJV). Jeremiah is only saying what many of us have already learned from personal experience. Habits that have been developed by consistent practice in the course of many years are hard to change. Habits have deep roots.

Daily decisions are so important because they affect your character. In reality, whoever you are right now is most likely who you are going to be to an even greater degree later in life. If you don't like the implications of that painful reality, now is the time to start making better decisions.

Decisions Have Serious Consequences

Decisions are important not only because they affect your character but also because they almost always have inescapable consequences. In the first chapter of Proverbs, Solomon described the fools of his age as those who hated knowledge, chose not to fear the Lord, respected none of Solomon's counsel, and despised his every rebuke (Proverbs 1:29-30). Of such people Solomon declared, "Therefore, they shall eat the fruit of their own way, and be filled to the full with their own fancies" (v. 31). He was basically explaining that people who hate God's Word and despise God's counsel will suffer the consequences that inevitably accompany that life choice. In fact, Solomon actually goes so far as to declare, "Because you disdained all my counsel, and would have none of my rebuke, I also will laugh at your calamity; I will mock when your terror comes" (vv. 25-26).

To some people, any talk about harsh consequences has the strange ring of being somewhat unchristian. After all, Christianity is the religion of forgiveness and second chances. It is a wonderful thing that sinners can be forgiven. Prodigals can always come home. The blood of Jesus is greater than all our sins. There is a reason we call the gospel good news – it *is* good news. But let me remind you that although sin can be forgiven, consequences cannot be avoided.

Paul explained it this way in Galatians 6:7: "Do not be deceived, God is not mocked; for whatever a man sows, that he will also reap." In other words, no matter how hard you try you cannot sin and avoid the consequences. Some negative consequences of sin will be experienced in this life. Others are reserved for the final judgment, but man will always have to face the painful consequences of sin.

King David stands out as the most powerful example of this principle. No other Bible personality better illustrates the fundamental truth that a man reaps what he sows. King David was a man after God's own heart, but in a moment of weakness he committed adultery with Bathsheba. In a failed attempt to cover up his sin, David also became guilty of deceit and murder. He eventually acknowledged his sin and was ultimately forgiven, but he still had to live with the painful consequences of his actions. He was given this message from

God, "Now therefore, the sword shall never depart from your house, because you have despised Me, and have taken the wife of Uriah the Hittite to be your wife" (2 Samuel 12:10).

The painful consequences of David's sin began with the tragic death of his infant son, but they clearly did not end there. His son Amnon raped David's daughter Tamar. Then Absalom, Tamar's brother, conspired to have Amnon murdered. Soon after that, Absalom was estranged from his father and then reconciled – but not fully. In the course of time, Absalom sought to win the hearts of the people and even tried, unsuccessfully, to usurp his father's throne. Eventually he was killed in battle. When David heard the news he wept, "O my son Absalom – my son, my son Absalom – if only I had died in your place! O Absalom my son, my son!" (2 Samuel 18:33)

David was forgiven, but he still had to endure the painful consequences of his sin. His family life was riddled with one problem after another including incest, rape, murder, rebellion and grief. I urge you to learn from this example. When God forgives, He removes the threat of spiritual punishment, but He does not rescue us from the natural consequences that come as a result of sinful choices.

For example, if you get drunk, you can be forgiven. But if you drive drunk, have a wreck and kill somebody, that decision will haunt you for the rest of your life. God will forgive the drunkenness, but He will not remove the legal and emotional consequences.

If you start experimenting with drugs and pornography, there is no doubt that God can forgive those sins, but you might have to battle an addiction to those habits for the rest of your life. Such addictions might negatively impact your marriage or career.

If you engage in sexual immorality, God can forgive that sin also, but you might have to deal with the consequences of sexually transmitted diseases, an unwanted pregnancy or a tarnished reputation.

Christians are serving time in prisons and penitentiaries all over this country. They have been washed in the precious blood of Jesus; they are forgiven, but they still have to pay their debt to society. The blood of Jesus does not wash away the negative and unwanted consequences that come as a natural result of regrettable decisions.

There was a girl I had the privilege to study with many years ago.

She obeyed the gospel by putting on Christ in baptism. She came up out of that water a brand new person. All of her sins were washed away, but she wakes up every morning and thinks about the baby she aborted when she was young, single and afraid. She is forgiven; but she still has to live with the painful memory of that lamentable decision. She has to live with regret and questions of what might have been for the rest of her life.

"Can a man take fire to his bosom, and his clothes not be burned? Can one walk on hot coals, and his feet not be seared?" (Proverbs 6:27-28). The answer to both questions is: "Absolutely not!" If you play with fire, you are going to get burned; if you experiment with sin there will always be painful and long-lasting consequences.

Decisions Determine Destiny

Decisions are important because they affect your destiny in life and in eternity. When I pull out of my neighborhood, turn west on Edmond Road, drive approximately two miles to MacArthur Boulevard, and turn south, I know from the very beginning of that road exactly where it is taking me. If I stay on that road for six miles, without deviating from my course, it will take me to my office at the North MacArthur Church of Christ.

You don't need a GPS to tell you that certain decisions are going to lead you away from God. When Achan took the devoted things after the battle with Jericho, how could he have expected things to turn out any differently than the way they did? He must have known from the very beginning how that decision would end. He had to know that he was taking a very precarious course in life and that acting as he chose could only end badly, just as it did. Achan and his entire family were executed (Joshua 7:24-25).

When Samson gave way to the affection of his heart and revealed the secret of his strength to Delilah, he had to have known, or at least suspected, the risk he was taking. She had betrayed him on three previous occasions. It is almost inconceivable to believe that this man could not have guessed the end from the beginning; yet he foolishly gave in to her nagging request. He told her the secret of his strength, and that reckless decision cost him his supernatural strength, his eyesight, his freedom and eventually his life (Judges 16).

I want to urge you not to make the same foolish mistake that Achan and Samson made. Don't fool yourself into thinking the road you are on will end somewhere other than where it is so obviously leading. If the path you are currently traveling is not taking you where you want to go, then the wisest thing you can do is change your direction now. Just remember this, when you pick a path in life you are also choosing a destination.

Jesus simplifies this truth by reminding us of only two roads in life: one is wide, and the other is narrow. Those two roads are leading to one of two destinations – destruction or life (Matthew 7:13-14). You are on one of those two roads. You are steadily moving toward one of those two destinies, and your decisions will direct you there.

Discussion Questions

1. Discuss how one key decision can change the direction of one's life.

2. How might small, insignificant decisions become life-changing?

3. How do habits help or hinder decisions?

4. How are we the sum total of our life decisions?

5. What can we learn from the decisions made by Judas, David, Samson and Achan?

Chapter 2

Personal Accountability

Good Over Evil –
Excellence Over Mediocrity

Decisions are important. They affect your character, they determine your destiny, and they often have serious consequences that cannot be removed even after your sin has been forgiven. If it is true that you are the sum total of every decision you have ever made and that you are exactly who you have decided to be, then something is very powerful about the freedom of choice. That freedom suggests that you do not have to be who you have always been. You have the power to change the direction of your life just by making different and better decisions.

Two decisions are absolutely essential if you hope to make real and lasting changes to your life. The first one is exemplified in God's extraordinary offer to King Solomon: "At Gibeon the LORD appeared to Solomon in a dream by night; and God said, 'Ask! What shall I give you?'" (1 Kings 3:5). It was a remarkable offer, and you can imagine how lesser men might have responded to such a proposition by asking for power, position, fame and fortune; it was the deal of a lifetime. But as you know, Solomon did not ask God for long life or riches; he did not ask for the life of his enemies (v. 11).

Solomon's prayer was humble and unselfish. "Therefore" he prayed, "give to Your servant an understanding heart to judge Your people, that I may discern between good and evil. For who is able to judge this great people of Yours?" (1 Kings 3:9). Solomon's prayer represents the first of two major decisions every faithful and growing Christian must make: the relentless determination to choose good over evil and right over wrong.

Good Over Evil

This first choice seems simple enough, but it is not as easy as it sounds. One reason it is so difficult to choose good over evil is because we are living in a culture that has embraced moral relativism. Proponents of this false philosophy claim that truth varies from person to person, from place to place and from time to time. If we are foolish enough to take our lead from today's culture, sometimes we feel as if we are shooting at a constantly moving target. What used to be wrong is now considered right, and something that is taboo in one place is culturally acceptable in another. Supposedly, what is right for one person might not necessarily be right for someone else. Of course, this approach to truth is completely inconsistent and absolutely absurd.

According to the one-chapter book of Jude, we are commanded "to contend earnestly for the faith" that has been "once for all delivered to the saints" (Jude 3). The definite article "the" is important. The faith Jude is talking about is not subjective or personal faith. He is not talking about my faith or your faith or someone else's faith; he is talking about objective faith and knowable truth. Jude is telling us that the complete system of Christian faith has been delivered to the saints once for all time, once for all people and once for all places. You can choose good over evil and right over wrong even if you live in a culture that has made such an ingenious attempt to deny or distort the truth. It is possible to make positive moral decisions because God's Word is forever settled in heaven (Psalm 119:89) and the truth as God has revealed it does not, will not and cannot change!

The second reason that it can be somewhat difficult to choose good over evil is because men have consistently tried to replace one for the other. Isaiah wrote, "Woe to those who call evil good, and good evil; who put darkness for light, and light for darkness; who put bitter for sweet, and sweet for bitter!" (Isaiah 5:20). We live in strange times. Men today seem willing to tolerate everything except perceived intolerance.

For instance, the strong effort to normalize or rationalize the sin of homosexuality is viewed by many to be virtuous, and, if you can believe it, even praiseworthy. However, if men and women of faith simply voice their biblical convictions on the subject, they are vilified in the arena of public opinion. When did that happen? When did it become wrong to do right and right to do something God's Word so plainly condemns as wrong? I suppose this has been happening since the days of Isaiah. There really isn't anything "new under the sun" (Ecclesiastes 1:9), but this is definitely another reason it can be so difficult for modern Christians to choose right over wrong and good over evil.

The third challenge in choosing good over evil arises when God's people adopt a defeatist attitude. Some Christians have failed so many times in the past they no longer believe it is possible to resist temptation. They have concluded temptation is irresistible and sin is inevitable. When such people are tempted, they are resigned to the idea that they must get drunk or get high or go online to look at inappropriate images; they can't resist the temptation to pass along a little gossip or to covet, lie or lose their temper. Many Christian people believe they are victims of temptation. Their "out of control behavior" is just that – out of their control, but such is simply not the case.

It might be hard to ignore temptation, but it is not impossible to resist it. According to Paul, "No temptation has overtaken you except such as is common to man; but God is faithful, who will not allow you to be tempted beyond what you are able, but with the temptation will also make the way of escape, that you may be able to bear it" (1 Corinthians 10:13).

God makes several promises in this passage, and you can trust His promises because He is indeed faithful. First of all, God promises that He will never tempt us beyond what we are able to bear. He also promises that along with every temptation there will always be a way out or a "way of escape." Finally, God promises that regardless of the intensity of the temptation "you can stand up under it" (1 Corinthians 10:13 NIV84). In other words, you can never say that you sinned because you were not able to overcome temptation. With every temptation, God has provided a way to escape. You don't have to take God's way out, but if you choose to sin you must admit it was your choice to do so.

There is a man in the congregation where I preach who, at one point in his life, was a raging alcoholic. His alcoholism was ruining his health, his marriage and his business. He was arrested seven times for driving under the influence. Finally a judge had the good sense to send him to Alcoholics Anonymous, and he was ordered by the court to attend the program. That brother has been clean and sober for the past 39 years. Think about that. He has been waking up every morning for the past 39 years and making the intentional decision not to drink. He is resisting temptation, and you can too. It is possible to choose good over evil and right over wrong.

The fourth reason it is so difficult to choose good over evil is because it is so much easier to shift the blame when we do wrong than it is to accept responsibility for the sin in our lives. Man has a history of shifting blame instead of accepting responsibility. This isn't something new; it is as old as the first man. When God confronted Adam about his decision to eat from the tree of the knowledge of good and evil, Adam's response was predictable. He said, "The woman whom You gave to be with me, she gave me of the tree, and I ate" (Genesis 3:12). When Eve was questioned her answer was somewhat similar, "The serpent deceived me," she said, "and I ate" (v. 13).

After the exodus, when Moses was on the mountain receiving the Law, Aaron made an image in the form of a calf (Exodus 32:4). When Moses confronted Aaron for bringing such a great sin upon the people, Aaron defended himself by shifting the focus onto the people he was supposed to be leading. "Do not let the anger of my lord become hot," he said and then explained, "You know the people, that they are set on evil" (v. 22).

Adam blamed God. Eve blamed the devil. Aaron blamed the people of Israel. Not one of them accepted personal responsibility. It must have been a refreshing change of pace for God to hear these words from King David, "Against You, You only, have I sinned, and done this evil in Your sight" (Psalm 51:4). David didn't blame God or the devil. He didn't try to defend himself by shifting the blame or pointing the finger at Bathsheba. In Psalm 51, David was basically saying, "God, this was my fault. I decided to sin against You. I decided to do what was evil in Your sight by taking another man's wife to be my own. It was my decision, and it is my fault."

David's example reminds me of a friend who responded to the public invitation. He informed me a few days in advance that he was having an affair and that he planned to confess that sin, repent of it and ask for the prayers of the congregation. He stood before the church that Sunday morning and made three brief statements; he said, "I have sinned against my God, I have sinned against my wife and I have sinned against my family." There is nothing commendable about the sin my friend committed, but you have to respect the fact that he took responsibility for his behavior. He didn't blame anyone else, and he certainly didn't blame God.

The reason personal accountability is so important is because you can never make significant changes in your character and personality until you admit to yourself that you are personally responsible for the mess you have made of your life. When you take ownership of poor decisions, stop shifting the blame and denying the truth, you can begin the difficult process of improving your character by making different and better decisions. You can change your life one day at a time and one decision at a time, but this will never happen if you are unwilling to take complete ownership of the mistakes you have made in the past.

The final challenge to choosing good over evil is the fact that we live in a generation that is so ungodly. Sin is so prevalent you don't have to go looking for it; sooner or later, if you sit still long enough, sin will find you. There have been times in more recent history that sin was most commonly practiced in the dark shadows of community life because people had the good sense to be ashamed of their evil behavior. Today, sin is practiced out in the open, without shame and without apology. For some reason it seems harder to do right when everyone else is doing wrong. It is so much easier to follow the crowd than it is to swim upstream or to cut across the grain; just because it is difficult does not mean it is impossible.

Take Noah as an example. Moses tells us that "Noah was a just man, perfect in his generations" (Genesis 6:9). The English Standard Version says that he was "blameless in his generation." The reason Noah is such a great example is because of what the Bible tells us about his generation. "Then the LORD saw that the wickedness of man was great in the earth, and that every intent of the thoughts of his heart was only evil continually. And the LORD was sorry that He had made man on the earth, and He was grieved in His heart" (Genesis 6:5-6). In addition to that, Moses tells us, "the earth was filled with violence" (v. 11) and "all flesh had corrupted their way on the earth" (v. 12).

Despite widespread corruption and violence, Noah was a blameless man who walked with God. If it was possible for Noah to do that in his generation, then you and I can do the same today. Doing the right thing might not always be easy – but it is always right. So don't do the easy thing just because it is easy. Do the right thing even when it is difficult and demanding. Decide now that you are going to be the kind of person who chooses right over wrong and good over evil. "Test all things; hold fast what is good. Abstain from every form of evil" (1 Thessalonians 5:21-22).

Excellence Over Moral Mediocrity

We began this chapter with Solomon's prayer for Israel, and we are going to end the chapter with Paul's prayer for the church in Philippi. Paul had an interesting habit of not just praying for people but also of telling those people the specific things he was asking God to do for them. He told the Philippians, "And this I pray, that your love may abound still more and more in knowledge and all discernment, that you may approve the things that are excellent, that you may be sincere and without offense till the day of Christ" (Philippians 1:9-10).

Paul's prayer represents the second major decision every faithful and growing Christian must make: the unwavering commitment to choose excellence over moral mediocrity. You see, the enemy of great Christian living is not always evil. Sometimes the enemy of great Christian living is what might be described as "good enough." In his song, "Rise Up, O Men of God," William P. Merrill challenges singers to "have done with lesser things" and to "give heart and mind and soul and strength to serve the King of kings." That thought has always been interesting to me. The hymnist did not say we should have done with sinful things. He said that we should have done with lesser things.

Some lesser things are not necessarily sinful, but the unwillingness to give up those things is keeping some of God's people from being as useful and as impactful as He would like for them to be.

Good people with enormous potential often fail to do great things, not because they lack the ability but because they have settled for good enough when something much better was possible. I hope you won't make that mistake. I hope you will strive to live a life of excellence by deciding not to settle for good enough when something immeasurably better is possible. Always strive to do your very best. God wants you to choose good over evil; but He also wants you to choose the best over the good enough.

Not long after I preached this series of lessons in Oklahoma City, an outstanding young Christian woman came to visit me in my office. She began by thanking me for the series of lessons about making better decisions and then proceeded to inform me that she had really taken the truth of God's Word to heart. In fact, she was so moved by the concept of choosing good over evil and the best over what some might consider good enough that she called off her engagement. She summarized her impressive decision with this simple explanation, "I don't think he is God's best for my life. I want someone who is going to strengthen my faith and help me get to heaven." Several years later, she became engaged to the kind of man that was truly best for her. I did their pre-marital counseling and was honored to officiate at the wedding. I think she would tell you that going through all the difficulty of extricating herself from a questionable engagement and waiting a few years longer for God's best was worth it in every way! She made this difficult and painful decision because she was seeking God's best for her life. I hope you will do the same. Don't settle for "good enough" when something better is possible.

The little poem "Sometimes" by Thomas S. Jones Jr. confronts every reader with a sobering thought:

> Across the years of yesterday
> He sometimes comes to me,
> A little lad just back from play –
> The lad I used to be.
>
> And yet he smiles so wistfully
> Once he has crept within,

I wonder if he hoped to see
The man he might have been.

It has a somewhat melancholy tone, but "Sometimes" makes us realize that at some point in the future, the person you now are is going to meet the person you will eventually become. That meeting has the potential to be somewhat disappointing, but it doesn't have to be. It could be an occasion for relief, contentment or possibly even great joy if you begin now to consistently choose good over evil and God's best over the merely good enough.

Discussion Questions

1. What role does the "Nature vs. Nurture" argument play in our decisions?

2. Who is responsible for my life choices – God, others who influence me, or myself? Explain.

3. Referring back to Chapter 1, is Judas to blame for his choice to betray Jesus even though Jesus' death was God's will?

4. Why do you think it's easier to blame someone else for your choices than to take personal responsibility?

5. What is moral mediocrity?

Chapter 3

God's Way Versus Our Way

Putting Aside Personal Desires

When I first began working in full-time ministry I was young enough to be the preacher and the youth minister. My wife and I traveled extensively with teenagers, took them to camps and retreats, and were blessed to teach many of their classes. On one occasion we had the opportunity to attend a very large gathering of more than 1,000 teenagers hosted on one of our university campuses. The main speaker at that event did an exceptional job of applying the Bible to teens and challenging them to bring their lives into conformity with God's will. Many young people responded publicly, expressing interest in baptism or confessing sin and asking for prayers. After the event, response cards were processed and passed along to local youth workers.

I remember sifting through the cards handed in by some of our teens and being somewhat shocked that one of our boys had written the following confession, "You name it; I've done it." I immediately started naming things and couldn't help wondering "Did he really do this or that or some other ungodly thing, really?" He was a deacon's son. He had grown up in a family of Christians who were devout in the practice of their faith. How was it possible for this young man who had such an outstanding heritage of faith to become entangled in so many sinful things? Why wasn't he making better decisions?

After nearly 20 years in ministry, I now realize that the gap between what Christians know and what they do is not strictly a youth-oriented problem. It is a challenge for every Christian regardless of age or maturity. There are adults who struggle with substance abuse. There are church leaders who are guilty of sexual misconduct and questionable financial practices. There are preachers and deacons and elders who sometimes wrestle with sinful habits that have to do with either their conduct or character. There is a vast difference between knowing the truth and living by it.

Pursuing Personal Desires

Sadly, it is possible to know a lot about the Bible without allowing that knowledge to have any measurable impact on the way you live or the decisions you make. Countless people claim to wear the name of Jesus, but not all of them follow His example or obey the moral teaching He has given us in the New Testament. Many are governed by much less-demanding standards. For instance, instead of following God's Word, some Christians make decisions based on their personal desires.

Paul spoke about such people in his letter to the Philippians: "For many walk, of whom I have told you often, and now tell you even weeping, that they are the enemies of the cross of Christ: whose end is destruction, whose god is their belly, and whose glory is in their shame – who set their mind on earthly things" (Philippians 3:18-19).

Some translations say "whose god is their appetite" (NASB). According to the MacArthur New Testament Commentary: "Appetite translates *koilia*, which refers anatomically to the abdomen, particularly the stomach. Here it is used metaphorically to refer to all unrestrained sensual, fleshly, bodily desires" (258). The people under consideration in this passage were being condemned because "they did not worship God but bowed down to their sensual impulses" and "their unrestrained pursuit of sensual pleasures" (258).

Such people have bought into the hedonistic worldview that pleasure is the highest good and proper aim of man. Unfortunately, even some of the people sitting next to you on Sunday morning have embraced this philosophy and are therefore preoccupied with self-gratification, whether by sex, drugs or alcohol. The prevailing attitude among such people is that "if it feels good, do it." Although certain things might feel good in the moment, the long-term impact of this approach to life causes one to become an enemy of the cross of Christ. Those foolish enough to start down this path seem dangerously unaware of sin's progressive nature and enslaving influence.

Paul described the awful mess people get into when they bow down to the god of personal desire. According to Paul, such people grow to a point of "being past feeling" and eventually give "themselves over to lewdness, to work all uncleanness with greediness" (Ephesians 4:19). Other translations shed even more light on this unfortunate state of existence explaining that those who "indulge in every kind of impurity" end up struggling with a "continual lust for more" (NIV84). Those who live for pleasure eventually reach a point at which they become "greedy to practice every kind of impurity" (ESV). The author of a book about spiritual warfare shared this graphic illustration of sin's progressive nature:

> While studying clinical psychology in graduate school several years ago, I ran across a photo in one of my textbooks of a young heroin addict that perfectly illustrated sin's addictive power. To satisfy his need, he had collapsed every vein in his arms, then his legs, and finally, through the course of depleting all other available spots, he had found the last. He lay in a doorway, dead, the hypodermic needle still in his tongue. It was an unpleasant yet graphic picture showing the end of every addictive sin. Not only are alcohol and drugs addictive; all sin is addictive. That same self-destructive behavior exists in all who allow the devil to deceive them to the point of having petrified hearts – no matter which route of temptation and sin they take. The end is spiritual destruction. (Joe Beam, *Seeing the Unseen* 26)

Conforming With the Crowd

Instead of looking to the Bible as their guide, some Christians follow their deadly and destructive desires while others end up mindlessly following the crowd. Biblically speaking, the majority can be, and often is, wrong. The crowd told Aaron, "Make us gods" (Exodus 32:1). The crowd crucified Jesus (Mark 15:14-15). They nailed the

Son of God to a cross. The crowd stoned the life out of Stephen (Acts 7:59). The crowd is on the broad path that leads to destruction (Matthew 7:13). No wonder God felt compelled to issue such a clear warning: "You shall not follow a crowd to do evil" (Exodus 23:2). We see this same warning presented with even greater detail in Proverbs 1.

> My son, if sinners entice you, do not consent. If they say, "Come with us, let us lie in wait to shed blood; let us lurk secretly for the innocent without cause; let us swallow them alive like Sheol, and whole, like those who go down to the Pit; we shall find all kinds of precious possessions, we shall fill our houses with spoil; cast in your lot among us, let us all have one purse" – my son, do not walk in the way with them, keep your foot from their path. (Proverbs 1:10-15)

The crowd makes the persistent appeal, "Come with us!" But the answer prescribed by divine wisdom is that we should not consent. We should not walk in the way with them. We should rather keep far from their path. Who could deny that a very large number of professed Christians simply ignore those warnings and trudge along behind the crowd wherever the crowd might happen to lead? Apparently it is easier to follow the crowd than it is to muster the moral courage necessary to stand against whatever the majority of people are practicing even when those practices are in conflict with Scripture, personal conviction and plain old common sense. For example:

> A few years ago psychologist Ruth W. Berenda and her associates carried out an interesting experiment with teenagers designed to show how a person handled group pressure. The plan was simple. They brought groups of ten adolescents into a room for a test. Subsequently each group of ten was instructed to raise their hands when the teacher pointed to the longest line on three separate charts. What one person in the group did not know was that nine of the others in the room had been instructed ahead of time to vote for the second-longest line.

Regardless of the instructions they heard, once they were all together in the group, the nine were not to vote for the longest line, but rather vote for the next-to-the-longest line.

The desire of the psychologists was to determine how one person reacted when completely surrounded by a large number of people who obviously stood against what was true.

The experiment began with nine teenagers voting for the wrong line. The stooge would typically glance around, frown in confusion, and slip his hand up with the group. The instructions were repeated and the next card was raised. Time after time, the self-conscious stooge would sit there saying a short line is longer than a long line, simply because he lacked the courage to challenge the group. This remarkable conformity occurred in about seventy-five percent of the cases, and was true of small children and high school students as well. (C. Swindoll, *Living Above the Level of Mediocrity* 225-26)

Sadly, we see something similar to this in the realm of Christian discipleship. In fact, John tells us that many people believed in Jesus, "but because of the Pharisees they did not confess Him" (John 12:42). Apparently, they were afraid that they might be put out of the synagogue; ultimately, according to John's testimony, "they loved the praise of men more than the praise of God" (v. 43). These timid and pitiful souls rejected Jesus, not for a lack of faith but because they did not have the moral courage to stand against the crowd. Many continue to make the same mistake today.

Following Our Feelings

Most Christians know that their conduct should be governed by the Word of God, but far too many continue to make major life decisions based on less reliable standards. They surrender to their own passion for pleasure, or they follow the crowd in doing wrong, or in many cases they simply follow their feelings. The problem with following feelings is that feelings are often deceptive and misleading.

John F. Kennedy Jr. crashed his private plane on the night of July 16, 1999. On that dark night, Kennedy apparently fell victim to what pilots call spatial disorientation. It is a sort of vertigo in which one loses all sense of what is up, down or level. One experienced pilot is quoted as saying, "It happens to all of us, you think the airplane is doing something it's not. You think the plane is turning right, but it is turning left." In the split seconds before Kennedy, his wife and sister-in-law died, he must have been totally confused. The reactions he made to what he was sensing apparently took him and his passengers into a near nose-dive into the ocean. Without proficiency in flying by his instruments, he was depending too much on his confused impressions.

How many of God's people are making the same terrible mistake? The book of Proverbs warns readers that "there is a way that seems right to a man, but its end is the way of death" (Proverbs 14:12). Jeremiah adds these words of caution, "The heart is deceitful above all things, and desperately wicked; who can know it?" (17:9). People who fly through life depending too much on their confused impressions are headed for a tragic and deadly crash.

Consider the biblical example of Uzzah. When the oxen stumbled on Nachon's threshing floor, it must have felt right for Uzzah to steady the ark of God. His reaction seems to have been spontaneous. Although the text says nothing about his motives, we can at least entertain the possibility that he was driven by the sincere desire to protect something sacred. He must have believed it was the correct course of action, but he learned the hard way that feelings can be dangerously misleading. According to the clear teaching of God's Law, it was not permissible for Uzzah to do what he did. Therefore, "the anger of the LORD was aroused against Uzzah, and God struck him there for his error; and he died there by the ark of God" (2 Samuel 6:7).

What if Uzzah had not relied upon his confused impressions? What if he had been more proficient at handling the guidance system of God's word? His head could have overruled his heart. His knowledge of Scripture could have governed his untrained feelings, and his story could have had a dramatically different outcome; but that is not what happened. The story as it stands is a warning to anyone who follows feelings instead of looking for "book, chapter and verse" instructions from God's Word.

Trusting Our Own Intellect

In the parable of the wise and foolish builders, Jesus made it clear that you can never go wrong when you base your decisions on the solid foundation of God's Word. Yet so many people are unwilling to let the Bible be their guide. Some follow the crowd, others follow their desires or their feelings, and still others follow what they perceive to be their superior intellect. There was a time when Israel had no king, and the last verse in the book of Judges tells us that "everyone did what was right in his own eyes" (21:25). People like that are still in the world today – people who make the mistake of thinking that they know better than God – that their way is more reasonable and more effective than His. Naaman is one such person.

Naaman was the commander of the army of the king of Syria. He "was a great and honorable man in the eyes of his master, because by him the LORD had given victory to Syria. He was also a mighty man of valor" (2 Kings 5:1), but he had leprosy. Fortunately, his wife had a servant girl from the land of Israel, and she told him about a prophet in Samaria who was able heal him. The king of Syria granted him permission to travel to Samaria, but when he finally found the prophet Elisha he was not pleased with the recommended cure.

> And Elisha sent a messenger to him, saying, "Go and wash in the Jordan seven times, and your flesh shall be restored to you, and you shall be clean." But Naaman became furious, and went away and said, "Indeed, I said to myself, 'He will surely come out to me, and stand and call on the name of the LORD his God, and wave his hand over the place, and heal the leprosy.' Are not the Abanah and the Pharpar, the rivers of Damascus, better than all the waters of Israel? Could I not wash in them and be clean?" So he turned and went away in a rage. (2 Kings 5:10-12)

Notice what the text tells us about Naaman. He said, "Indeed, I said to myself." In other words, Naaman put a great deal of thought into what he expected Elisha to do. That was his biggest mistake. He thought he knew better than Elisha, and by extension he thought he knew better than God. He thought Elisha was going to stand over him, call upon the name of the Lord, and wave his hand over the place where his body had been infected by leprosy. When Elisha did not behave the way Naaman thought he should, it made him angry. He couldn't make a logical connection between dipping seven times and being cured of leprosy, and he did not understand why he had to dip in the Jordan instead of doing the same thing in the more preferable rivers of his homeland. Many people continue to make the same mistake today.

Why do people baptize infants, say a sinner's prayer, or ask Jesus into their hearts instead of being baptized for the remission of their sins? They think they know better than God. Why do some church leaders add instruments to their worship services and permit women to have an expanded role in the public assembly? They think they know better than God. Why have some mainstream denominations begun to welcome practicing homosexuals into their fellowship instead of teaching them to repent and turn to God? They think they know better than God.

When it comes to making life-altering decisions that influence our eternal destiny, we should not obey the cravings of our own sinful desire. We should not follow the crowd in doing wrong. We should not let our feelings be our guide. We should not presume to imagine that our ways are somehow wiser than God's. Instead, we should humble ourselves and acknowledge along with Jeremiah that "it is not in man who walks to direct his own steps" (Jeremiah 10:23). Solomon said it best, "Trust in the LORD with all your heart, and lean not on your own understanding; in all your ways acknowledge Him, and He shall direct your paths" (Proverbs 3:5-6).

Discussion Questions

1. What role does pleasure play in decision-making?

2. What insight does Matthew 7:13-14 give us about decisions?

3. The Bible clearly shows us the effects of crowd mentality in the crucifixion of Christ and the stoning of Stephen. How do you see crowd mentality at work? In society? In the church?

4. Uzzah's story demonstrates how following our feelings can get us into trouble. What insight into following our feelings does Proverbs 14:12 suggest?

5. Why do you think people trust in their own "wisdom" rather than God's wisdom?

Chapter 4

Going by "the Book"
Bible-Based Decisions

The call of God can be alarming, confusing and sometimes even amusing. For instance, God called Abraham to offer his beloved son Isaac as a burnt offering (Genesis 22:2); that's alarming. He called Hosea to marry an adulterous wife (Hosea 1:2); that's confusing. He called Ezekiel to pack his bags and leave the city through a hole in the wall (Ezekiel 12:4-5); that's somewhat amusing. In Jeremiah 35, He called His faithful prophet to do something extremely unusual. He commanded him to "go to the house of the Rechabites, speak to them, and bring them into the house of the LORD, into one of the chambers, and give them wine to drink" (Jeremiah 35:2). Though Jeremiah might not have fully understood the lesson God was preparing to teach, he still did what God commanded him to do.

> Then I set before the sons of the house of the Rechabites bowls full of wine, and cups; and I said to them, "Drink wine." But they said, "We will drink no wine, for Jonadab the son of Rechab, our father, commanded us, saying, 'You shall drink no wine, you nor your sons, forever. You shall not build a house, sow seed, plant a vineyard, nor have any of these; but all your days you shall dwell in tents, that you may live many days in the land where you are sojourners.' Thus we have obeyed the voice of Jonadab the son of Rechab, our father, in all that he charged us, to drink no wine all our days, we, our wives, our sons, or our daughters, nor to build ourselves houses to dwell in;

nor do we have vineyard, field, or seed. But we have dwelt in tents, and have obeyed and done according to all that Jonadab our father commanded us." (Jeremiah 35:5-10)

What God requested of Jeremiah sounds strangely inappropriate to modern believers; but we should bear in mind that God anticipated the outcome. He was familiar with this family, and He knew that their father Jonadab had commanded them not to drink wine. He knew in advance that they would refuse to drink, and He was using their example to teach an important object lesson. He commanded Jeremiah:

"Thus says the LORD of hosts, the God of Israel: 'Go and tell the men of Judah and the inhabitants of Jerusalem, "Will you not receive instruction to obey My words?" says the LORD. "The words of Jonadab the son of Rechab, which he commanded his sons, not to drink wine, are performed; for to this day they drink none, and obey their father's commandment. But although I have spoken to you, rising early and speaking, you did not obey Me. I have also sent to you all My servants the prophets, rising up early and sending them, saying, 'Turn now everyone from his evil way, amend your doings, and do not go after other gods to serve them; then you will dwell in the land which I have given you and your fathers.' But you have not inclined your ear, nor obeyed Me. Surely the sons of Jonadab the son of Rechab have performed the commandment of their father, which he commanded them, but this people has not obeyed Me."' Therefore thus says the LORD God of hosts, the God of Israel: 'Behold, I will bring on Judah and on all the inhabitants of Jerusalem all the doom that I have pronounced against them; because I have spoken to them but they have not heard, and I have called to them but they have not answered.'" (Jeremiah 35:13-17)

God spoke to the people of Judah, but they refused to listen; He called to them, but they did not answer. God continues to speak today. He does so through His inspired Word, but the people of this generation, as was pointed out in the previous chapter, are not listening to

Him as they should. They are too busy following their sinful desires, their feelings, their intellect or the multitude of people who, in many cases, do not know their left hand from their right. If decisions have significant consequences, if they really do affect character and determine destiny, then we must make better decisions, and the only way to do that effectively is to seek guidance from the Bible.

The Word of God

The most obvious reason we should make Bible-based decisions is because the book we call the Bible is the Word of God. When Jesus was tempted to turn stones into bread He responded by quoting Scripture to Satan, He said, "Man shall not live by bread alone, but by every word that proceeds from the mouth of God" (Matthew 4:4). According to Jesus, the words of the Bible come directly from God's mouth. The Bible may be human in penmanship, but it is divine in authorship: "holy men of God spoke as they were moved by the Holy Spirit" (2 Peter 1:21). The words are God's words. When you open the Bible, you are reading the very mind of God in human language.

God's people, then and now, may not always be willing to listen, but He has been relentless in His attempts to communicate. In fact, He has gone to extraordinary lengths to make His will known to man. Listen to the first two verses of the book of Hebrews:

> God, who at various times and in various ways spoke in time past to the fathers by the prophets, has in these last days spoken to us by His Son, whom He has appointed heir of all things, through whom also He made the worlds. (Hebrews 1:1-2)

When God spoke in the past, He spoke directly "to the fathers." He spoke to men like Abraham (Genesis 12:1-2), Isaac (26:2-3) and Jacob (32:28). He spoke "by the prophets" like Isaiah (Isaiah 6:9-10), Jeremiah (Jeremiah 1:9-10) and Micah (Micah 1:1-2). He spoke "at various times." He spoke at the very beginning of Creation saying, "Let there be light" (Genesis 1:3). He spoke to Adam and Eve in the Garden of Eden and gave them instructions concerning the tree of the knowledge of good and evil (2:15-17). He spoke to Noah prior to the flood that destroyed the ancient world and commanded him to build an ark (6:5-7, 13-14). He spoke to Moses about the exodus of Israel (Exodus 3:9-10). He spoke to Joshua during the conquest of the Promised Land (Joshua 1:6-7). He spoke to Gideon during the time of the judges (Judges 6:14). He spoke to Samuel when Israel demanded a king (1 Samuel 8:7-9). He spoke to Solomon at the height of Israel's glory days (1 Kings 3:5, 11), and he spoke to John the Baptist to prepare the world for the coming of Christ (John 1:33).

Not only did God speak to the fathers by the prophets at various times, He also spoke to them "in various ways." God was creative in His persistence. He spoke to Moses from a burning bush (Exodus 3:2). He spoke to Israel from atop a fiery mountain (19:18-19). He spoke to Elijah in a still small voice (1 Kings 19:12). He spoke to King Belshazzar through the handwriting on the wall (Daniel 5:5), and He spoke to Balaam through a dumb donkey (Numbers 22:28). The history of God's effort to communicate with man is both awe-inspiring and in some cases ridiculous, but when you put all of these efforts together you cannot miss the obvious conclusion. God has spoken, and He still speaks to men today through His Son.

The appropriate response to the Word of God was summarized by Eli when he gave the following instructions to Samuel, he said "Go, lie down; and it shall be, if He calls you, that you must say, 'Speak, LORD, for Your servant hears'" (1 Samuel 3:9). The number one reason to make Bible-based decisions is because the Bible is the Word of God. It is, as some have described it, the Maker's manual. Our Lord has spoken, and He continues to speak. Unlike the people of Judah in Jeremiah's day, we should listen to Him.

Our Guide to Salvation

We should read the Bible and do what it says because the Word of God teaches us how to be saved. In Paul's second letter to Timothy, he reminded his young friend that from the very earliest days of his life he had been privileged to know the Holy Scriptures that are able to make one "wise for salvation" (2 Timothy 3:15).

When we open the New Testament to the book of Acts, we see that the preaching of God's Word led to the salvation of about 3,000 souls in one day (Acts 2:41). It led to the salvation of many others including Saul of Tarsus (9:18), a Roman centurion named Cornelius (10:47-48), a businesswoman named Lydia (16:15), a Philippian jailer (v. 33), an Ethiopian eunuch (8:38), Simon the sorcerer (v. 13) and the synagogue ruler Crispus (18:8). The Word of God made each and every one of those people wise for salvation!

Somebody might ask, "Why should I bother reading a book that is thousands of years old?" The answer should be fairly obvious. This book is from God, and if you study it, if you really take the time to dig into the truth as it has been revealed from heaven you can find the answer to the world's most important question, "What must I do to be saved?" The Bible reveals the answer to that question. The Word of God makes people wise for salvation; that's what it did in the past, and that is what it continues to do today. That's why James commanded his readers to "get rid of all moral filth and the evil that is so prevalent and humbly accept the word planted in you, which can save you" (James 1:21 NIV84). The Word of God can save your soul.

Our Guide for an Effective Life

Immediately after pointing out to Timothy that the Bible makes a man wise for salvation, Paul went on to explain that "All Scripture is given by inspiration of God, and is profitable for doctrine, for re-proof, for correction, for instruction in righteousness, that the man of God may be complete, thoroughly equipped for every good work" (2 Timothy 3:16-17). It is clear from what Paul wrote that we should read the Bible and do what it says not only because it teaches us how to be saved but also because the Word of God equips us for greater effectiveness in life.

According to Paul the Scripture is "profitable" because it teaches, corrects, rebukes and trains in righteousness. Pay close attention to the "so that" statement in verse 17, "So that the man of God may be thoroughly equipped for every good work" (NIV84). The phrase "man of God" is commonly understood as being a direct reference to one who speaks for God (a prophet in the Old Testament and an evangelist in the New). In context, Paul is speaking to a young evangelist explaining to him how he can be a good minister. There is, however, a sense in which the Word of God does the same thing for every Christian that it does in the life of a preacher. It equips us for life. It fully equips us for every good work.

There isn't anything God has called us to do that the Bible does not equip us to do successfully. This is true of all our various relationships. This is true of marriage and family and parenting. It applies to our work and our finances. It applies to becoming a Christian and worshiping faithfully. It includes our mission of world evangelism. No matter what God has called us to do, the Bible can prepare us to do it successfully. "His divine power has given to us all things that pertain to life and godliness" (2 Peter 1:3). Everything we need to be successful or effective in this life God has revealed through His inspired Word.

Joshua was an important leader of God's people in the Old Testament. In fact, God worked through this young man to bring Israel into the land of Canaan. Listen to the advice God gave Joshua when he took over the reins of leadership from Moses; He said:

> Only be strong and very courageous, that you may observe to do according to all the law which Moses My servant commanded you; do not turn from it to the right hand or to the left, that you may prosper wherever you go. This Book of the Law shall not depart from your mouth, but you shall meditate in it day and night, that you may observe to do according to all that is written in it. For then you will make your way prosperous, and then you will have good success. (Joshua 1:7-8)

If you have a Bible, then you have access to a truly prosperous life, but you have to meditate on the Word of God. You have to read the book, and you have to be careful to do everything written in it. If you follow God's Word faithfully and do not turn from it to the right hand or to the left, like Joshua, you will have "good success." The Lord will equip you for every good work.

Our Guide for Judgment Day

The Bible teaches us how to be saved, and it equips us to live successfully and effectively; but there is still one more reason to make

Bible-based decisions. The Bible is the only book that can adequately prepare us for the judgment day. Jesus put it this way:

> And if anyone hears My words and does not believe, I do not judge him; for I did not come to judge the world but to save the world. He who rejects Me, and does not receive My words, has that which judges him – the word that I have spoken will judge him in the last day. (John 12:47-48)

People tend to reject and ridicule the Bible, but they really need to be reading the Bible because it will be the standard of God's judgment. We cannot afford to ignore the parts we don't like, especially the parts that point out sin in our lives. We do not have the luxury of editing God's Word for content. That is what King Jehoiakim tried to do; he cut out the parts he didn't like and threw them into the fire (Jeremiah 36:23), but that did not change the will of God or prevent Him from carrying out judgment on His people.

The New Testament book of James provides us with a healthier and more helpful approach to the Bible. James compared the Word of God to a mirror that not only shows our true reflection but also helps us to see what we ought to be and what we still can be if we are willing to do the hard work of making Bible-based decisions. This is what he said:

> For if anyone is a hearer of the word and not a doer, he is like a man observing his natural face in a mirror; for he observes himself, goes away, and immediately forgets what kind of man he was. But he who looks into the perfect law of liberty and continues in it, and is not a forgetful hearer but a doer of the work, this one will be blessed in what he does. (James 1:23-25)

When my son, Ryder, was 8 years old, he used to play basketball in the living room. There was one time that he brought a laundry basket down from his bedroom and set it up as his goal. At one point, he was standing next to my chair with his back to the basket throwing the ball over his head. I was somewhat impressed because although he missed the target on three consecutive attempts he didn't miss by very much and the ball was landing in the exact same spot each time. On his fourth attempt, just before he shot the ball, he stopped and said, "I know!" Then he ran over to the goal and moved it less than a foot in the direction where his previous shots had landed. He came back to my chair, turned his back, threw the ball and made it dead center into the basket.

I was immediately struck by the fact that he found it easier to move the target than to adjust his aim. I fear that many Christians are tempted to do the same thing. Sin is just another word for "missing the mark," and plenty of modern Christians have decided that instead of adjusting their aim they would rather move the target. I strongly urge you not to make that mistake. Instead of tampering with the target, adjust your aim. In the inspired words of James, "Be doers of the word, and not hearers only, deceiving yourself" (1:22).

Discussion Questions

1. Abraham, Hosea and Ezekiel were all asked by God to do things we would find strange. Would you have made the same decisions they did? Why?

2. What experience was Jesus referring to in Matthew 4:4?

3. In what creative ways did God choose to speak to His people? How does He speak to us today?

4. How would you respond to someone who says, "Why should I bother reading a book that is thousands of years old?"

5. If the Bible is our guide for living an effective life, how important is the translation we use?

Chapter 5

To God Be the Glory

God-Glorifying Decisions

The French philosopher, André Maurois, asked, "Why are we here on this puny mud heap, spinning in infinite space?" In answer to his own question, he confessed, "I have not the slightest idea, and I am quite convinced that no one else has the least idea." As Christians, we not only have an idea but we also have a firm conviction. The Bible tells us where we came from (Genesis 1:27), where we are going (John 14:1-4), and exactly what God wants us to do while we are here. According to Paul we are here on earth "to the praise of His glory" (Ephesians 1:12). We are here to give God glory in the church and in Christ Jesus our Lord (3:21).

In His Sermon on the Mount, Jesus commanded His followers, "Let your light so shine before men, that they may see your good works and glorify your Father in heaven" (Matthew 5:16). The question for Christians is not "Why are we here?" The question for us is, "How do we do what God has put us here to accomplish, and how do we give glory to God by the lives we live and the decisions we make?" There is probably no limit to the number of ways that we could answer that question, but I would like to suggest at least five.

Following God's Standards for Sexual Purity

We can glorify God by following His standards for sexual purity. In the previous chapter on Bible-based decisions, it was pointed out that the Bible is God's Word, and that His Word not only teaches us how to be saved eternally (2 Timothy 3:15) but that it also teaches us how to live here and now (vv. 16-17). When it comes to the subject of sexual purity, God's Word is not silent. In fact, God is very clear about His standards for sexual purity. He tells us the truth about fornication, adultery, homosexuality and drunkenness. He warns us in the most direct terms that those who do such things will not inherit the kingdom of God (1 Corinthians 6:10). Just a few verses later the Lord commands us to "flee sexual immorality" (v. 18). He goes on to explain:

> Every sin that a man does is outside the body, but he who commits sexual immorality sins against his own body. Or do you not know that your body is the temple of the Holy Spirit who is in you, whom you have from God, and you are not your own? For you were bought at a price; therefore glorify God in your body and in your spirit, which are God's. (1 Corinthians 6:18-20)

Joseph is an excellent example of glorifying God in your body by fleeing sexual immorality. After his brothers sold him into slavery he was carried away to the land of Egypt where he was sold to Potiphar, an officer of Pharaoh and a captain of the guard (Genesis 39:1). The Bible tells us that "Joseph was handsome in form and appearance" (v. 6) and that "his master's wife cast longing eyes" on him (v. 7). Her sexual advances toward this young man were not subtle. She was aggressive in her pursuit of him. In fact the Bible tells us that "she spoke to Joseph day by day" (v. 10), and on one occasion she actually "caught him by his garment" and said, "Lie with me" (v. 12). Joseph was under intense pressure, but he responded with wisdom, discretion and courage.

The Word of God tells us that Joseph "did not heed her, to lie with her or to be with her" (Genesis 39:10). In other words, Joseph not only resisted temptation by rejecting her illicit advances but he also did everything within his power to remove himself from her presence. He refused to be alone with her. When that approach did not work, Joseph fled and got out of the house leaving his garment in her hands (v. 12). The wonderful thing about this story is that we are not left to wonder what prompted Joseph to do what he did. At one point, Joseph asked Potiphar's wife, "How then can I do this great wickedness, and sin against God?" (v. 9).

The choice Joseph made was costly. He ended up being falsely accused (Genesis 39:14-15) and unfairly imprisoned (v. 20), but he refused to sin against God. He glorified God in his body, and his story is here to remind us that we must do the same in spite of the pressures we are under or the consequences we might have to face. There are standards we must always follow and lines we must never cross. Compromise is not an option. By the way, running from sexual sin is not a sign of weakness or cowardice; it is a testimony to moral courage and spiritual strength. When we can no longer resist temptation, we should run from it. That's what Joseph did. Anyone who is interested in glorifying God will make the same decision.

Modeling God's Pattern for Marriage

We can glorify God by modeling His pattern for marriage. Marriage was God's idea. It was God who said, "It is not good that man should be alone; I will make him a helper comparable to him" (Genesis 2:18). God is the one who took a rib from Adam's side and created Eve. God is the one who said, "Therefore a man shall leave his father and mother and be joined to his wife, and they shall become one flesh" (v. 24). It was Jesus who said, "Therefore what God has joined together, let not man separate" (Matthew 19:6).

Because marriage was divinely instituted, it is subject to divine rules and regulations. God set forth those regulations in language we can all understand. He made it clear that His fundamental plan for marriage included a heterosexual, monogamous, lifelong relationship. However, in spite of God's original intent, marriage has fallen on hard times. Not only have strong efforts been made to redefine marriage, but commitment to marriage also seems to be at an all-time low.

Although marriage counselors may be very helpful, and they have said and written many good things about marriage, people cannot make their marriage all that it could and should be without the benefit of biblical instruction. The Bible provides answers to some of the most basic problems that arise in marriage. Paul reminds us in his letter to the Ephesians that God's plan requires both love and respect. "Nevertheless," he said, "let each one of you in particular so love his own wife as himself, and let the wife see that she respects her husband" (5:33). Paul also points out that God's plan calls for submission and sacrifice. Look closely at what he wrote:

> Wives, submit to your own husbands, as to the Lord. For the husband is head of the wife, as also Christ is head of the church; and He is the Savior of the body. Therefore, just as the church is subject to Christ, so let the wives be to their own husbands in everything. Husbands, love your wives, just as Christ also loved the church and gave Himself for her. (Ephesians 5:22-25)

Paul has basically given us the four ingredients to a happy and successful marriage. Marriage will never be all that God wants it to be without love, respect, submission and sacrifice. Dan and Geri Walker are founding members of the North MacArthur Church of Christ in Oklahoma City. They were married on Jan. 20, 1957. They were married for 57 years at the time of Geri's death in 2014. When you meet people who have been married that long, it is sometimes hard to envision what they were like in the early years of their life together. Just 13 years into their marriage, on Christmas Day 1970, Geri wrote the following note to her beloved husband:

My Husband,

I searched to find a gift that would tell you how much I love you and at last I realized there just wasn't one. So here I give you my Christmas gift.

I give you my admiration, my trust, my support, my devotion, and my unending love for the rest of our life together.

I will try my best to be the wife you need. I will try to make our home a place of comfort from the world outside. A place you will want to come to.

You tell me I am beautiful when I smile. I promise to smile often. Please on those days that I don't, hold me close and understand.

You are my world and I pray I will be worthy of you. If I displease you in any way, tell me and I will change.

I realize my gift is small but it is all I have to give that is mine. I give it freely. My life spent loving and making you happy. Thank you for the happiest Christmas I can remember.

Your Wife

Geri respected and submitted to her husband, and Dan loved and sacrificed for his wife. I mentioned that they were married in 1957. I feel safe in assuming that on that day, Dan made the vows that most men make on their wedding day. He vowed to love, honor and cherish her. He promised to forsake all others. He promised for richer or poorer, for better or worse, in sickness and health, till death do us part. I am proud to tell you that Dan kept his promise.

When Geri was diagnosed with Alzheimer's, Dan took care of her at home as long as he could, and when her needs became greater than what he could meet without assistance he found the very best place to meet her needs. He visited her every single day and would often sing to her. Dan and Geri had a beautiful life together. She joyfully submitted to him. He willingly sacrificed for her. That kind of love is a choice you make every day, and when two people spend a lifetime sacrificing for and submitting to one another the result is a rare and lovely thing that not only models the biblical pattern for marital success; it also glorifies God. If we are serious about making God-glorifying decisions, we must follow God's standards for moral purity, and we must strive to model His pattern for Christian marriage.

Living Worry-Free Lives

We can glorify God by living worry-free lives. Paul commanded the Christians in Philippi to "be anxious for nothing, but in everything by prayer and supplication, with thanksgiving, let your requests be made known to God; and the peace of God, which surpasses all understanding, will guard your hearts and minds through Christ Jesus" (Philippians 4:6-7). According to Paul, Christians can worry more and pray less, or they can pray more and worry less. The choice is yours, but let me warn you that the worried Christian is a universal disappointment. I've got to confess that those last few words hurt because much like Martha I am often "worried and troubled about many things" (Luke 10:41).

A little over three years ago, my family moved to a new neighborhood. I was very anxious throughout the entire process. At one point, our real estate agent, who makes no profession of the Christian faith, chastised me in front of my family. She basically told me that my obvious anxiety about the whole "buying and selling" process was a negative reflection of my faith in God. I don't remember her exact words, but she was basically saying "If your God is so great and your faith in Him is so strong, then why do you worry so much about little things?"

The experience was painful, embarrassing and revealing. I am not proud of my poor example, but I am sharing it here to remind you that the world is watching. People will not respect our fear and anxiety, but they will be impressed when we live with confidence knowing that the same God who feeds the birds of the air and dresses the lilies of the valley can take care of all of our needs and any of our unexpected emergencies. When we live with peace that passes understanding, the world will be amazed and God will be glorified.

Overcoming Evil With Good

We can glorify God by overcoming evil with good. In Matthew 5, Jesus commanded His listeners to "love your enemies, bless those who curse you, do good to those who hate you, and pray for those who spitefully use you and persecute you" (v. 44). In keeping with the same spirit of Christ, Paul issued this simple but challenging command to the Christians at Rome; he said "Do not be overcome by evil, but overcome evil with good" (Romans 12:21). The Christian response to hatred is not more hatred, and the Christian response to evil is not greater evil. According to Jesus, we must overcome evil with good by our stubborn and resilient determination to live a life of love.

On the morning of April 19, 1995, Timothy McVeigh parked a truck full of explosives in front of the Alfred P. Murrah Federal Building in Oklahoma City. Susan Walton, a sister in Christ, was in the federal employees' credit union on the third floor when the bomb exploded. She was found under a filing cabinet and a door frame. Both her legs were broken; she had a basal skull fracture, nerve damage behind both eyes and a broken nose. She lost six teeth; her jaw was fractured in six places; she had a ruptured spleen; and her legs were crushed from the knees down.

She was in the hospital for five weeks and in rehab for three weeks before she finally got to go home. She has endured 26 surgeries after the bombing. Her mobility has been permanently hampered, and she goes through bouts of chronic pain, but she has not allowed herself to become a prisoner to bitterness, self-pity or hatred. In fact, after Susan recovered from her extensive injuries she started a non-profit organization called Suited for Success. The organization provides women from low-income backgrounds with two interview-appropriate outfits in order to build confidence and more adequately suit them for success as they strive to enter the job market. They suited their first client on Aug. 1, 1997. According to suitedforsuccess.com, they had served more than 7,800 women as of 2014.

Susan did not choose to suffer through such a terrible tragedy, but after being victimized by hatred and cruelty she did make the choice not to be overcome by evil. She chose instead to overcome evil with good. That decision has helped nearly 8,000 women. It has inspired many Christians to follow the difficult and demanding example of Jesus, and it has contributed to the praise of God's glory.

Confronting Death

We can glorify God by confronting death with faith and courage. I think it is important to point out that Christians can glorify God not just by how they live but also by the way they die. Our fear of death says something about our faith. It says that we don't really believe death is just another word for victory. It says that we might not really believe that Jesus has prepared a place in His Father's house that is better than anything we have ever experienced in this life. It might even give unbelievers the idea that we haven't really taken God at His word when it comes to our personal salvation.

My wife's granddaddy went into the hospital on Thursday, May 29, 2008. He had an emergency surgery on Friday. On Monday, June 2, the doctors informed him that he had stage four lung cancer. When those doctors walked into his room, we were discussing his recovery; when they walked out of his room, we were preparing ourselves for his death. On Thursday, June 12 (just two weeks after entering the hospital), he was gone. As he gazed out into eternity, he did not tremble with fearful uncertainty; he spoke with confidence. These are some of the last things he said to his family:

I don't know how anyone could go through this without the church and without faith. I love my Lord, and my God is real. My God is real. It's time for this old man to go home. I'm not afraid; everything is going to be all right. I'm not scared. I'm just waiting for Jesus to open the door!

Granddaddy died with calm assurance and confident expectation because his anchor was rooted firm and deep in the Savior's love. He knew that he was making the final journey from life to eternity, but he also believed that he did not have to make that journey alone because our God is real, and He has promised to be with us for the last mile of the way (Psalm 23:4).

This is not a book about modern moral issues, marriage, worry or suffering and death. This book is about improving our character and determining our destiny by making better decisions. But if we are truly serious about doing that, we will make decisions that honor and glorify God. We will follow God's standards for sexual purity. We will model His pattern for marriage. We will strive to live worry-free lives. We will overcome evil with good. We will confront death with faith and courage. By doing such things, we will glorify our Father who is in heaven.

Discussion Questions

1. What does it mean to glorify God?

2. How do we know that Joseph really trusted God's demand for sexual purity? See Genesis 39. How did his decision glorify God?

3. Discuss Paul's four ingredients to a successful marriage.

4. How would you describe the peace that passes understanding?

5. If you have known someone in the final stages of death, did he or she glorify God in those moments? How?

Chapter 6

Act Like Jesus
Christ-Imitating Decisions

"**W**hat is the measure of success to the Christian?" This question was asked in a Sunday morning adult Bible class. A variety of answers was given, but one stood out from all the rest. One of the students, a retired minister, said, "Success for the Christian is to act like Jesus without having to think about it." Can you imagine having so absorbed the image, the mindset and the motives of Christ, that you act like Him without having to think about it? For most Christians, that goal remains a constant challenge, but if spiritual success is truly measured by Christlikeness, then how can we begin to make decisions that reflect that holy ambition? What would it look like to make Christ-imitating decisions?

Numerous answers could be given because the Lord has so many characteristics that are worthy of our imitation, but four attributes seem to stand out from the rest.

Imitating Christ's Love

Christ-imitating decisions begin with the greatest love. In the story about the rich young ruler, Mark gives this important detail: "Then Jesus, looking at him, loved him" (Mark 10:21). The young man in that story was unwilling to give up his material wealth to follow the Lord, but in spite of his unhealthy affection for material things, Jesus still looked at him with love. Three times in his gospel account John makes reference to the disciple whom Jesus loved (John 20:2; 21:7, 20). He also tells us that "Jesus loved Martha and her sister and Lazarus" (11:5). When Jesus came to Bethany after the death of Lazarus, He saw Mary weeping. The inspired text tells us that "He groaned in the spirit and was troubled" (v. 33). The shortest verse in the Bible says that "Jesus wept" (v. 35). Those fortunate enough to be there to witness divine tears streaming down human cheeks exclaimed, "See how He loved him!" (v. 36).

Jesus loved the rich young ruler. He loved John. He loved Martha, Mary and Lazarus. Jesus loved people, and that love found its fullest expression at the cross. He hinted at this to His disciples when He told them, "Greater love has no one than this, than to lay down one's life for his friends" (John 15:13). Reflecting on that remarkable sacrifice, Paul was right to conclude He "loved me and gave Himself for me" (Galatians 2:20). If we are serious about being more like Jesus, then we must learn the secret of sacrificial love. In fact, this kind of love is the number one identifying mark of Christian discipleship. Jesus put it this way, "A new commandment I give to you, that you love one another; as I have loved you, that you also love one another. By this all will know that you are My disciples, if you have love for one another" (John 13:34-35). The world will know that we are what we claim to be if and only if we love one another.

Corrie ten Boom is an excellent example of how demanding it can be to love others with the love of Jesus Christ. Corrie is a survivor of the Holocaust. She and her family were imprisoned for housing Jews during the war. She suffered much cruel treatment in the concentration camps and lost several members of her family. If anyone ever had a reason to hate her enemies, Corrie did. But in her book *The Hiding Place*, she tells the story of how the love of Christ is more powerful than the cruelest hatred.

Corrie and her sister Betsie witnessed unspeakable atrocities. One day, they watched as a guard brutally beat one of the feeble-minded inmates. Corrie asked her sister, "What can we do for these people? Afterward I mean. Can't we make a home for them and care for them and love them?" Betsie answered, "Corrie, I pray every day that we will be allowed to do this! To show them that love is greater!" Later that morning, Corrie realized that while she had been thinking of the feeble-minded inmates, her sister was thinking of their persecutors (ten Boom, 204).

The first time I read that story, it made me cry, not just because of the unfair persecution or intense suffering this family was subjected to, but because I realized that I am not nearly enough like Jesus. The thought of loving such contemptible people never entered my mind; it didn't enter Corrie's either and that's the point. Most of us, like Corrie, are eager to love the downtrodden, the sick and the less fortunate, but very few Christians think like Betsie – very few love like Jesus. The love of Christ demands more than simply loving the lovable. It prompts us to do what is best for other people even when they don't deserve it, even when that love comes at great personal expense. That's what Jesus did for us. That's what we must do for others if we want to be like Him.

Imitating Christ's Humility

Christ-imitating decisions require the rarest humility. It seems somewhat awkward and out of place to describe the omnipotent, omniscient and omnipresent God as humble, but that is exactly what the Bible says about Jesus. There could have been no incarnation without this irreplaceable ingredient. Paul explained it in these memorable words:

> Let this mind be in you which was also in Christ Jesus, who, being in the form of God, did not consider it robbery to be equal with God, but made Himself of no reputation, taking the form of a bondservant, and coming in the likeness of men. And being found in appearance as a man, He humbled Himself and became obedient to the point of death, even the death of the cross. (Philippians 2:5-8)

A quick look at the life of Christ reveals uncommon humility. Jesus came from heaven to earth; He is the God who became man and the Creator who entered into His own creation. He is God wrapped in swaddling cloth in the manger; God washing the dirty feet of proud disciples; God arrested by an angry mob; God on trial before mere men; God being scourged, brutally beaten, spit upon, mocked, ridiculed and publicly humiliated. He is God being nailed to the torturous tree, God dying for the sins of all mankind. He is the Master who became the servant of all and the Author of life who willingly suffered death. How could He do it? The answer is humility.

In May 2014, people across the nation were talking about NBA player Kevin Durant's MVP acceptance speech in which he thanked everyone who contributed to his success as a person and as a player. He thanked team owners, front office personnel, coaches, teammates, members of the training staff, friends and fans. Then, as he was thanking family members, he locked eyes with his mother and called her the real MVP. The thing that was so amazing about that speech is not just the humility of Durant but how little we expect humility from professional athletes and how surprised we are to see this characteristic where we least expect it.

As refreshing as his demonstration of humility was, it is just as discouraging when we look for humility in places where it ought to be and don't find it there. Church leaders sometimes get more credit than they deserve. Preachers who are used to being told how great they are might just be tempted to believe it, but we should all be careful to remember there is no greater contradiction than a proud Christian. In fact, it is impossible to be proud and Christlike at the same time. Yet how often do we see modern leaders who seem unable to disengage from the very same dispute that sidetracked the earliest disciples: the question as to who among them should be considered the greatest.

We might think Jesus permanently laid that argument to rest when He washed the disciples' feet (John 13:5) or when He so clearly explained that "he who is greatest among you shall be your servant" (Matthew 23:11). But we are still confronted with Christian leaders who seem to do almost everything out of bitter envy and selfish ambition, the very motives that are described in Scripture as "earthly, sensual, demonic" (James 3:15). In the inspired language of James, "My brethren, these things ought not to be so" (v. 10).

If we are truly serious about bearing the image of Christ, then we have to stop making excuses for ugly ambition, petty pride and sinful self-centeredness. We need to follow the same instructions Paul gave to the Christians in Philippi when he wrote, "Let nothing be done through selfish ambition or conceit, but in lowliness of mind let each esteem others better than himself. Let each of you look out not only for his own interests, but also for the interests of others" (Philippians 2:3-4).

Imitating Christ's Compassion

Christ-imitating decisions express the deepest compassion. Earlier in this chapter I mentioned the shortest verse in the Bible, "Jesus wept" (John 11:35). Some have a hard time understanding why Jesus wept when He had already determined to resurrect His dead friend, but that story gives us a glimpse into the multifaceted nature of God. How sad would it be if we were forced to choose between a God who weeps for the broken-hearted or a God who can raise the dead?

Thankfully, we are not forced to make that choice because the one true God not only has the power to raise the dead but He also has the compassion to weep for those who weep. That great balance between God's love and God's power is a tremendous blessing, but it also confronts us with an incredible challenge. Christlikeness requires a willingness on our part to enter into the mess that others sometimes make of their lives; it demands a willingness to feel the pain that others are experiencing. This is what Jesus did so naturally during His earthly ministry:

> Then Jesus went about all the cities and villages, teaching in their synagogues, preaching the gospel of the kingdom, and healing every sickness and every disease among the people. But when He saw the multitudes, He was moved with compassion for them, because they were weary and scattered, like sheep having no shepherd. (Matthew 9:35-36)

The Greek word translated "compassion" means "to have the bowels yearn." It is a visceral reaction that expresses the idea of sympathy and pity. As Jesus saw the physical and spiritual suffering of the multitudes, His heart went out to them. It was a gut-wrenching response to the brokenness, grief and pain that surrounded Him. He saw the weariness of the multitudes. He saw the burdens that weighed them down, and He felt pity for them because they were like sheep without a shepherd.

In the conclusion of our Lord's parable about the unmerciful servant, the forgiving master asked the unforgiving servant a revealing question, "Should you not also have had compassion on your fellow servant, just as I had pity on you?" (Matthew 18:33). The application is obvious. Because we are the beneficiaries of God's compassion, we, more than anyone else, ought to be compassionate to the physical suffering and spiritual brokenness of our fellow human beings.

When I was about 25 years old and about six months into full-time ministry, I was called to the home of Don and Abbie Smith. Don had been sick for quite some time and was dying. When I walked into that room, his wife was lovingly stroking his brow. He had three adult daughters. One of them was holding his right hand, one of them was holding his left hand and the other one was holding his feet. They stayed there by him until he died.

That experience was a lesson for me. I noticed people calling to check on the family. I noticed people discreetly coming into that home with food. I watched people hug them and cry with them and suffer along with them in the pain of their loss. What I saw that day and what I have seen many times since is the image of Christ reflected in the compassion of His church. Weeping with those who weep allows the world to see the glory of Jesus reflected in our lives.

Imitating Christ's Forgiveness

Christ-imitating decisions extend the fullest forgiveness. The forgiveness of God is all-encompassing. In the first of his three letters, John assures us that "if we walk in the light as He is in the light, we have fellowship with one another, and the blood of Jesus Christ His Son cleanses us from all sin" (1 John 1:7). Two verses later he said that "If we confess our sins, He is faithful and just to forgive us our sins and to cleanse us from all unrighteousness" (v. 9). The blood of Jesus does not cleanse us from *some* of our sin or *most* of our sin. His blood cleanses us from all sin. God's forgiveness is comprehensive and complete. That is why we can sing these wonderful words written by Horatio Spafford from his song, "It Is Well With My Soul":

My sin – O, the bliss of this glorious tho't –
My sin, not in part but the whole,

Is nailed to the cross and I bear it no more:
Praise the Lord, praise the Lord, O my soul!

Forgiveness is such a wonderful thing to receive, but as Christians we are not just called to receive forgiveness; we are required to dispense it as well. Jesus is the best example of what this looks like and how demanding it can be. Jesus had the authority to forgive sins on earth, and He exercised that authority (Matthew 9:1-6). He told the sinful woman in Luke 7:48, "Your sins are forgiven." He told the woman caught in the act of adultery, "Neither do I condemn you; go and sin no more" (John 8:11). Jesus was a forgiving man, and the most convicting example of this particular aspect of His nature can be seen most clearly at the cross.

Matthew offers the most detailed account of what His enemies did to Him. They laid hands on Jesus (26:50) and spat in His face and beat Him (v. 67); they struck Him with the palms of their hands (v. 67) and had Him bound, led away and delivered to Pontius Pilate (27:2). When Pilate made it possible for Jesus to be released, they chose Barabbas instead (v. 21) and actually cried out for Jesus' life saying things like, "Let Him be crucified!" (v. 22) and "His blood be on us and on our children" (v. 25). Because of this bloodthirsty crowd Jesus was scourged and crucified (v. 26).

Along with all of the horrible things done to Jesus, the people also said some terrible things as well. They hurled insults at Him and ridiculed Him as He hung there dying. What was our Lord's response to all of this cruel treatment and hateful mockery? He prayed for their eventual forgiveness: "Father, forgive them, for they do not know what they do" (Luke 23:34). Offering forgiveness to people who don't deserve it might be the greatest challenge to our pursuit of Christlikeness, but that pursuit is incomplete without it.

I pulled into the church parking lot early one morning and found one of my closest friends pacing by the front door. I don't know how long he had been waiting for me, but he was clearly agitated and I soon found out why. His wife had confessed that she was having an affair. He was devastated. The whole family was hurt. We met on and off for months. He talked. I listened. We prayed. During one of our many counseling sessions, he told me that she wanted to come home. I remember asking him, "What are you going to do?" I will never forget his answer. He said, "Tim, this is my best opportunity to show her the love of God." He forgave her. He took her back, and they are still together to this day.

We sometimes sing, "Let the beauty of Jesus be seen in me." That song forces us to think seriously about what others see when they take a closer look at the decisions we make and the lives we lead. It reminds me of a funny memory that took place early in my marriage and ministry. The day after our wedding, my wife and I moved into a little three-bedroom house right across the driveway from the Mount Vernon Church of Christ. There was a garage behind the house that had two storage units connected to it. We came home one night to find the doors of both of those units swinging open in the wind. We initially thought we had been robbed, but then I remembered that the lady who cleaned the church building almost always had her son and daughter with her. The very next time I saw that little boy I asked him if he had been playing in our storage area.

He took a deep sigh of relief and then proceeded to tell me, "I thought you were going to ask if I was looking in your windows." That raised an entirely new concern I had not previously considered. Apparently he was playing in the storage units behind my house, and he was looking in my windows. In fairness to that little boy, his behavior was innocent. He had been playing on the elevated driveway between our house and the church building and from that vantage point he could see into our kitchen.

Nonetheless, if we claim to be the modern-day disciples of Jesus Christ, then people have a right to look into the window of our personal spiritual lives to see if we practice what we preach, to see if we intend to be what we pretend to be and to see if our beliefs have any real impact on the decisions we make. Because that is the case, let us be all the more careful to make Bible-based, God-glorifying and Christ-imitating decisions.

Discussion Questions

1. A popular book in 1896 was titled *In His Steps* and had as its theme the question, "What would Jesus do?" In your opinion, is that a reachable goal or an unrealistic ideal?

2. What is the secret of sacrificial love?

3. Why is humility so important when it comes to serving Christ (Matthew 23:11)?

4. Name some ways the church can show compassion to those in the community.

5. Is the statement "I forgive you, but I won't forget" truly a reflection of forgiveness?

Chapter 7

Top Priority
Kingdom-Seeking Decisions

I met Harvey Childress during the summer of 1996 when He was working with the Waterview Church of Christ in Richardson, Texas. In 2001, Harvey wrote a book called *The Riches of Love* where he talked about the incredible impact one verse from the New Testament had on his life; that verse was Matthew 6:33, "But seek first the kingdom of God and His righteousness, and all these things shall be added to you."

Harvey was just a little boy when he learned that passage, but he decided he was going to start seeking first the kingdom of God. The preacher from Harvey's home congregation encouraged him to become a gospel preacher. Despite the fact that he was scared to death of public speaking, he went to the great Northwest and established congregations of the Lord's church all over that part of the country. He was instrumental in establishing York College and served as the first president of that school. When I met him, he was in his 90s and was still busy serving the Lord. He was the director of a ministry the Waterview congregation called "Strengthening Mission Churches." It was a ministry that sent teaching materials to small, struggling churches all over the United States and some foreign countries.

Think about all of the things this man did with his life. He was a preacher, church planter, Christian college president and friend to missionaries and small churches. He did all those things with his life because when he was just a small boy the words of Matthew 6:33 were deeply impressed on his heart. This one inspired verse captivated his imagination and had an immeasurable impact on the decisions he made for the rest of his life. What about you? How might this one simple command to "seek first the kingdom" change your life? Would following it more consistently cause a shift in any of your values or require that you reorganize some of your priorities? To help you think more seriously about the potential impact of kingdom-seeking decisions, I want to challenge you to consider three questions that might prove to be uncomfortably revealing.

Seeking the Kingdom in Our Finances

Question #1: Is the kingdom first when it comes to how you spend your money? When I was preparing for ministry at Oklahoma Christian University, it was my privilege to meet and befriend Avon Malone. His father, Joe Malone was a commercial artist, but later in life he was converted and became a preacher. Joe did what some have referred to as "chalk talks." He would literally draw a picture as he preached from the Word of God. I have two books in my personal library that are filled with some of the pictures Joe drew. My favorite depicts a man being baptized. His whole body is submerged beneath the water but one arm remained above the surface; the man's hand was firmly clutching his wallet. Apparently, he was willing to give everything he had to the Lord – everything that is, except his money.

As a young preacher, I did not feel comfortable preaching on the biblical subject of money. It made me extremely nervous to preach what the Bible says about the grace of giving. That fear was a symptom of spiritual immaturity. As I have grown in my love for Christ and His kingdom, I have become much more comfortable and confident. I now have no reservation when it comes to talking about money because I have grown to understand that giving is really more about love than anything else.

According to a well-known illustration, a preacher once wrote a wealthy and influential businessman requesting a contribution. The preacher received a blunt refusal which ended by saying, "As far as I can see this Christianity business is just one continual give, give, give." After a brief moment of reflection, the preacher wrote the following reply, "I wish to thank you for the best definition of the Christian life I have ever heard." Christianity is a giving religion.

God gave (John 3:16), Jesus gave (Galatians 2:20), and each one of us must give if the kingdom is truly first in our lives.

When it comes to making kingdom-seeking decisions, love is not satisfied with daily minimum requirements. Love does not ask "how little" but rather "how much" can I give. That's why King David refused to offer a burnt offering to the Lord that cost him nothing (2 Samuel 24:24). That's why the widow in Luke 21, "out of her poverty put in all the livelihood that she had" (v. 4), and that's why the churches in Macedonia gave "according to their ability" and "beyond their ability" (2 Corinthians 8:3). When we love the kingdom of God more than anything else, we will give as we have prospered (1 Corinthians 16:2). In fact, love for the kingdom will motivate us to give willingly, joyfully and sacrificially because that's what love does. Love inspires us to count the cost and pay the price.

Seeking the Kingdom With Our Time

Question #2: Is the kingdom first when it comes to how you spend your time? You can tell a lot about people by how they spend their time. Some people wake up unbelievably early and sit in a boat or in a tree stand all day long and even late into the night. You couldn't pay me enough to sit in the woods on a cold day or on a dark night. Forget about it! Why do some people spend so much time walking through the woods or floating on a lake? They love the outdoors, and they love to fish and hunt. People are always eager to spend time doing what they love.

That is how I used to be with basketball. I used to play as much basketball as I could squeeze into a day. I spent almost every week of my summer vacations at basketball camps in the Pocono Mountains in Pennsylvania. I used to shovel snow off the basketball court in my backyard in the wintertime just so I could play a little basketball. When I wasn't playing basketball, I was watching it on television or reading about it in a magazine. It dominated my time because I loved it.

I remember reading about a businessman who was working 10-12 hours a day, six days a week, and then he started working on Sundays too. There is only one reason why somebody would spend that much time working. That man loved his job. He loved all the prestige that came with his position, and he loved all the things he could buy with the money he was making from spending all that time at work. He loved what he was doing; that's why he invested so much of his time into his profession.

I distinctly remember hosting a gospel meeting with Willie Franklin when I was still working with the church in Mount Vernon, Mo. That was one of the longest weeks of my life. We got up early each morning and spent all day visiting delinquent members and trying to make contact with potential prospects for evangelism. Willie spoke every night, and after each sermon we stayed at the church building visiting with members and meeting privately with people who wanted to study the Bible. Some people just wanted to share their struggles, and they wanted Willie to encourage them and pray with them. There were nights we stayed at the church building until after midnight and then were up bright and early the next morning to do it all over again.

It was a great week, but I was absolutely exhausted at the end of it. I remember sitting in my driveway the morning after the meeting. Willie and I were visiting about the week. At one point in that conversation, I asked him "Willie, brother, how do you do it? How do you go so hard every day without sleep, and you never seem to get tired?" Without the slightest hesitation, Willie looked at me and said, "Tim, if anything ever happens to my wife I don't plan to ever get remarried. If I ever lose my wife I will go night and day for Jesus!" Do you know why he said that? He made that statement because people spend time doing what they love the most. Willie loves God, and he loves Jesus, and he loves sharing the gospel more than anything else in this world.

What do you love? Can you honestly say that you love God and are seeking first His kingdom when you are too busy to read the Bible or to pray – but you always have plenty of time to watch your favorite TV programs? Can you say that you are seeking first the kingdom when you decide to do something other than attend regularly scheduled worship services and Bible studies, something as mundane, for instance, as sleeping in? Are you seeking first the kingdom of Christ when it is more important for you to attend a ballgame than it is to support a gospel meeting? Or when you spend time on the golf course when you could be volunteering for VBS or some other ministry of the local church? What you do with your time and money says a lot about your priorities. It may say more about you than you would like to admit.

Seeking the Kingdom in Our Conversations

Question #3: Does the kingdom come first in your conversations? In Matthew 12:34, Jesus said, "For out of the abundance of the heart the mouth speaks." This passage is profoundly and sometimes painfully true. Jesus is telling us in this passage that if you listen to a man long enough he will tell you what he treasures and values more than anything else. Our words really are that revealing.

Most of us have been around friends or acquaintances who are always talking about how much money they make, the new house they just bought, the new car they are driving, or the expensive vacation they have planned for the summer. I'm not trying to judge anybody too harshly, but Jesus made it clear that we can pretty much tell what is in a person's heart if we listen closely enough. If a person is constantly talking about money and the things money can buy, that is what they cherish in their hearts.

If you ever get stuck next to a devoted grandmother on an airplane, buckle up for the long haul because she is going to tell you about every cute or funny thing her grandchildren have ever done. Parents and grandparents talk about their children and grandchildren because that is what fills their hearts. The same thing is true about a sports fanatic. You might be wondering why you have never heard some people talk about anything except their favorite professional sports team. Every time you talk with certain people, it seems like the only thing they want to talk about is baseball, football or basketball. From the overflow of the heart the mouth speaks.

That makes me wonder why it is so difficult to get modern Christians to include Jesus in the conversations they are already having with fellow students, co-workers, friends and family members. The modern church seems to be working desperately hard to encourage members to speak up and put in a good word for Jesus and the gospel. But when you read the Bible you notice that the enemies of God's people in the past couldn't get the earliest disciples to be quiet. Consider just a few examples from the book of Acts:

> So they called them and commanded them not to speak at all nor teach in the name of Jesus. But Peter and John answered and said to them, "Whether it is right in the sight of God to listen to you more than to God, you judge. For we cannot but speak the things which we have seen and heard." (Acts 4:18-20)

> And when they had brought them, they set them before the council. And the high priest asked them, saying, "Did we not strictly command you not to teach in this name? And look, you have filled Jerusalem with your doctrine, and intend to bring this Man's blood on us!" (Acts 5:27-28)

> So they departed from the presence of the council, rejoicing that they were counted worthy to suffer shame for His name. And daily in the temple, and in every house, they did not cease teaching and preaching Jesus as the Christ. (Acts 5:41-42)

> At that time a great persecution arose against the church which was at Jerusalem; and they were scattered throughout the regions of Judea and Samaria, except the apostles … Therefore those who were scattered went everywhere preaching the word. (Acts 8:1, 4)

Let me tell you why these men never stopped talking about God and why they never stopped preaching the gospel of Jesus Christ. They kept on talking about God, the Son of God and the kingdom of God for the same reason other people talk about sports or hobbies or politics or family or money – that's what was in their hearts. The reason people talk about the things they talk about is because that is what they treasure and that's what they value more than anything else. What does that tell you about your priorities, and what really comes first in your life?

For many years now, I have had a little Calvin and Hobbes comic strip pinned to the bulletin board in my office. It records the following conversation between Calvin and his imaginary friend, a stuffed tiger named Hobbes. Calvin begins the conversation by asking, "Hobbes, do you think our morality is defined by our actions or by what is in our hearts?" Hobbes answers truthfully and honestly by saying, "I think that our actions show what is in our hearts." More than a little ticked off, Calvin replies, "I resent that!"

Calvin wanted to separate his actions from his values; he wanted to separate what he did from who he was. The problem is we just can't do that. Whether we like it or not, our actions declare to the world the truth about who we are, what we value and what is in our hearts. Before you move on to the next chapter, do a little inventory of your checkbook, calendar and conversations. How do you spend your time? How do you spend your money? What is the most recurring theme in the majority of your conversations? As you think about those three questions, remember what Jesus said, "But seek first the kingdom of God and His righteousness, and all these things shall be added to you" (Matthew 6:33).

Discussion Questions

1. What do you think it means to seek the kingdom of God first?

2. If you actually put the kingdom first, how would that affect your money, time and conversations?

3. What does it mean to give as we have prospered? Is that a certain dollar amount? Why or why not?

4. List some ways you can spend your time seeking first the kingdom of God.

5. Why is it so difficult for modern Christians to include Jesus in their conversations? Compare that to the attitude of the disciples discussed earlier in this chapter.

Chapter 8

Do Unto Others

Golden Rule-Guided Decisions

As we begin this chapter let's consider the ground covered up to this point. In Chapter 1, we learned decisions are important because they affect character, they often have significant consequences, and they determine our eternal destiny. In Chapter 2, we discussed the importance of choosing good over evil and excellence over moral mediocrity. From that point on we have explored some of the challenges and benefits involved with making Bible-based, God-glorifying, Christ-imitating and kingdom-seeking decisions. Although these four standards should definitely equip us to make better decisions, some might be wondering if it wouldn't be easier to have one simple rule to guide us through this messy and difficult process.

If that's how you feel, I have good news for you. Jesus has given us a rule for making better decisions. He has given us a rule that should guide and govern all of our inter-personal relationships. Most people call it the Golden Rule; it's found in Matthew 7:12. Toward the end of what has been described as the Sermon on the Mount, Jesus said, "Therefore, whatever you want men to do to you, do also to them, for this is the Law and the Prophets."

There you have it – one simple rule that everyone can follow. All you have to do is ask yourself how you want to be treated and then use the answer to that question as the guideline for how you treat everyone else. Most of us are familiar with this rule; we understand it, and in some cases we have even taught it to others – but that's not the real challenge. The challenge for every Christian is to apply this rule and allow it to transform all of our various relationships. For the remainder of this chapter, consider five specific areas where this rule could be and probably should be applied.

The Golden Rule in Business

The Golden Rule should guide and govern our business dealings. As Christians, we sometimes make the mistake of compartmentalizing our lives. We have our family life, work life, social life, recreational life, academic life and then somewhere in the mix of all our other activities we find time for our Christian life. The problem with that approach to Christianity is that Jesus has never consented to being just one spoke among the many other spokes in the wheel of your life. In reality, Jesus insists upon being the very hub of your life which means no compartments are off limits to Him. When Jesus is the hub of your life, He affects every spoke. That means you are no longer just a husband and father; you are a Christian husband and father. You are no longer just a wife and mother; you are a Christian wife and mother. You are no longer just a friend and neighbor; you are a Christian friend and neighbor. For the particular point under consideration in this chapter, you are no longer just a boss or an employee; you are a Christian boss and employee. Unfortunately, not all who wear the name of Jesus practice the Golden Rule in their business dealings.

For instance, it is not unheard of for teenage Christians who work as waiters or waitresses to let their friends eat for free. I remember a boy in our youth group who worked for the local video store. He never charged his friends. They knew if he was working, they could borrow a movie without paying. He was being extremely generous, but he was doing so at someone else's expense. Behavior like this is not the norm, but it does exist among some Christian teenagers. As much as I hate to admit it, this is not strictly a youth-oriented problem. Some adults do not seem to understand that permanently "borrowing" something from the office is the same as stealing. Others charge their employer for work they haven't done, or they claim time on their timesheet that they haven't actually worked, or they overcharge on their expense accounts to line their own pockets.

If you were a business owner, how would you want your employees to treat you? Most of us would want to be treated with honesty, integrity and fairness. Doesn't the Golden Rule demand that you treat your boss or business owner the same way? The principle, of course, applies in reverse as well. Employers should treat the people who work for them the way they want to be treated. If employers want to be treated with dignity, kindness, trust and respect, that is how they should treat those who work for them. Christian salesmen who follow the Golden Rule should never brag about taking advantage of someone in a business transaction. They should treat people the way they want to be treated even when they might not profit as much as they could have if they were not operating under this divine principle.

J.C. Penney seemed to have a strong grasp of this concept. The original J.C. Penney stores did not open under that name. Instead, Penney named them for his philosophy of business. They were called the Golden Rule Stores. Penney offered the following rationale:

> In setting up a business under the name and meaning of the Golden Rule, I was publicly binding myself, in my business relations, to a principle which had been a real and intimate part of my family upbringing. To me the sign on the store was much more than a trade name. We took our slogan, 'Golden Rule Store' with strict literalness. Our idea was to make money and build business through serving the community with fair dealing and honest value. (Maxwell, *There's No Such Thing as "Business" Ethics* 67)

Apparently, Penney believed one simple rule made every business decision rather simple: "Just as you want men to do to you, you also do to them likewise" (Luke 6:31). Christian business owners, employers, managers, salespeople and employees should take this example to heart; they should allow the Golden Rule to guide and govern all of their business transactions.

The Golden Rule in Our Personal Boundaries

The Golden Rule should also assist Christians in the somewhat difficult struggle to set appropriate sexual boundaries. The idea of saving sex for marriage might seem antiquated to the world, but it should not be seen that way to those who belong to Jesus. With that thought in mind, think about the moral implications of the Golden Rule. If you are a Christian woman and you hope to marry a Christian man, you want that man to save himself for you and for you alone. If you expect him to preserve his virginity and maintain his purity until he says the words "I do" on your wedding day, the Golden Rule demands the same level of purity from you. If that's what you expect from your future husband, that's what you ought to do for him. The Golden Rule should guide and govern the boundaries you set in this most intimate area of your personal life.

It is not unusual for the world to approach this subject with an unfair double standard but that standard does not apply to members of God's church. Sexual sin is just as sinful for men as it is for women; it's just as shameful too. What does that mean for single men who are reading this book? It means that if you hope to marry a Christian woman and you want that woman to save herself sexually for you and only you and you expect her to preserve her virginity and maintain her purity until she walks down the aisle and gives herself away to you, the Golden Rule won't allow the world's double standard. The Golden Rule demands that you keep yourself pure for your future wife.

Let's shift this discussion out of the realm of dating and move it into the arena of marriage. The Word of God teaches us that "marriage is honorable among all, and the bed undefiled; but fornicators and adulterers God will judge" (Hebrews 13:4). Several years ago, at a lectureship, I heard an older preacher challenge Christian men with these words: "Be a one-woman man with your eyes, with your thoughts, and with your body." Every Christian husband should strive to follow that advice not just because adulterers will be judged but because they understand and appreciate the implications of the Golden Rule. Husbands should be faithful with their thoughts, eyes and bodies because they know how devastating it would be if their wives were not faithful to them in any one of these three vital areas.

Remember this important question, "How do you want to be treated?" Answer that question honestly, and then allow your answer to serve as a guideline for how you treat the person you are dating or the person you have married. In other words, don't forget to rely on the Golden Rule when it comes to setting proper boundaries for sexual purity.

The Golden Rule in Our Speech

The Golden Rule should not only guide our business relationships and moral standards; it should also govern what we say about other people. The inspired book of James addresses this subject frequently and forcefully. In the very first chapter of the letter, James tells readers: "If anyone among you thinks he is religious, and does not bridle his tongue but deceives his own heart, this one's religion is useless" (James 1:26). In chapter 3, in what might be the Bible's most powerful and comprehensive teaching on taming the tongue, James described the tongue as small (v. 5), powerful (vv. 2-4), destructive (vv. 5-6), unruly (vv. 7-8) and incredibly inconsistent (vv. 9-10). In chapter 4 he issued this straightforward command, "Do not speak evil of one another, brethren" (v. 11).

Despite these inspired insights, many Christians continue to struggle with the devastating and divisive sins of gossip and slander. This is most likely the case because "the words of a talebearer are like tasty trifles, and they go down into the inmost body" (Proverbs 18:8). There is something so sinfully satisfying about gossip that some Christians find it irresistible. If this is one of your besetting sins, please consider how the Golden Rule might apply to this area of your life. Abraham Lincoln has been credited with saying that you should "never add the weight of your character to a charge against another person without knowing it to be true," but I'd like to suggest that even if we know certain information to be true, the Golden Rule should restrain our natural impulse to pass along such information. If sharing what we know about another person, even if it is true, has the potential to hurt or humiliate that individual, the Golden Rule applies.

As you wrestle with the concept of how the Golden Rule ought to govern what you say about others, consider the following illustration. A preacher once asked a woman in his congregation to scatter feathers down a certain street in their small town. When she returned, he then instructed her to retrace her steps and gather up all the feathers she had scattered. The woman replied, "That is impossible. The wind has scattered them in all directions!" The preacher proceeded to make this point: "So it is with your words of gossip and slander; they have been carried away like feathers in the wind and it is impossible to call them back."

Before you share the intimate details of another's personal struggle or moral failure, bear in mind that you can never gather up your words once they leave your mouth and remember what Jesus said, "Just as you want men to do to you, you also do to them likewise" (Luke 6:31). If there are certain things you wouldn't want other people to say about you, determine not to pass along the same kind of information about them.

The Golden Rule in Spreading the Gospel

The Golden Rule is much more far-reaching and applicable than most Christians have taken the time to consider. Along with everything already noted, the Golden Rule should inspire evangelistic zeal. A young mother took her son to his first parade. She got caught up in the festivities, and her son wandered off into the crowd. Fearing the worst, she began a frantic search for her lost son. Eventually, she found him marching along at the end of the procession. He was lost, and he didn't even know it.

We meet people like that little boy every day. They are marching through life without a care in the world. They are lost, but they just don't realize it. What does the Golden Rule require us to do for such people? Doesn't it obligate us to share the gospel with them? This is going to make some people very uncomfortable because some find evangelism extremely intimidating, but please take a few minutes to think about this scenario.

What if you hadn't grown up in a Christian family? What if you never had Christian parents and grandparents and Bible class teachers? What if you were lost, without hope and without God in the world, and you knew something was painfully lacking in your life, but you didn't know what it was? What would you want people with a saving knowledge of the gospel to do for you? Wouldn't you want them to share their saving knowledge? Isn't there a specific way in which you would want them to do that?

Most of us would not appreciate being ridiculed, intimidated or manipulated. If we were lost, we would want others to tell us the truth, but we would most likely prefer that they do so in love (Ephesians 4:15). We would want them to share their saving hope with "gentleness and respect" (1 Peter 3:15 ESV), and we would want them to preach God's Word with "complete patience" (2 Timothy 4:2 ESV) understanding that it takes some people longer than others to comprehend the plan of salvation. If that is the case, and I believe it is, doesn't the Golden Rule require that we do for others the same thing we would want them to do for us?

Are you doing that? If not there could be a very uncomfortable confrontation awaiting you on the day of judgment. In fact, one of the most disturbing hymns we sing describes the potential encounter between a child of God and a friend or acquaintance who died without ever hearing the gospel of Christ. In his song titled "You Never Mentioned Him to Me," James Rowe describes that painful encounter:

> When in the better land before the bar we stand,
> How deeply grieved our souls will be;
> If any lost one there should cry in deep despair,
> "You never mentioned Him to me,"
>
> You never mentioned Him to me,
> You helped me not the light to see;
> You met me day by day and knew I was astray,
> Yet never mentioned Him to me.

The proper application of the Golden Rule could spare you from the pain, discomfort, regret and embarrassment of having any such encounter, and much more importantly, it can inspire you to have the kind of spiritual conversations every Christian should be having before it is everlastingly too late.

The Golden Rule in Our Giving

Finally, the Golden Rule should guide and govern our benevolent activity. We know that pure and undefiled religion includes visiting orphans and widows in their affliction (James 1:27), and we understand that when we see a brother or sister "naked and destitute of daily food" it is not enough to say "be warmed and filled" if we do not also "give them the things which are needed for the body" (2:15-16). Most Christians understand the idea expressed by Jesus in Matthew 25 where He said, "Inasmuch as you did it to one of the least of these My brethren, you did it to Me" (v. 40), but it is not enough to feed the hungry, give a drink to the thirsty, clothe the naked and visit those who are sick and imprisoned just because we understand that concept. We should also be motivated by the Golden Rule.

What if you were hungry, thirsty, cold and lonely, sick and imprisoned? What would you want other people to do for you? That question is so fundamental, but unfortunately it sometimes takes hardship and suffering to make us realize our responsibility to others. I received a phone call late one night. It was one of those calls that if you have been in ministry very long you know that it can't be good. When the phone rings that late at night, it is either a wrong number or something bad has happened.

I can't remember who made the call, but I do remember what the person said. A young man had been trying to rope cattle from the back of a pick-up truck and he fell out, hit his head and was in the hospital in a coma. I got up, dressed and made the 40-minute drive to the hospital. Others came that night; they came early the next morning, and they kept coming. In the difficult and uncertain days that followed, I don't think that young man's parents were ever alone. Weeks later as his condition stabilized, I had a long visit with his parents.

They fought back tears and confessed, "We didn't know. The thought never occurred to us how much it would hurt to go through something like this and how much it would mean to us to have such incredible support from our Christian family. The next time something like this happens to someone else we are going to be there for them just as so many people have been here for us." What were they saying? They were basically admitting that they were going to start practicing the Golden Rule. Having learned how important it is to receive loving support from Christian friends, they were committing themselves to do the same for others. That sounds much like what Jesus said, "Just as you want men to do to you, you also do to them likewise" (Luke 6:31).

It is hard to choose good over evil consistently and God's best over the merely good enough, but Jesus has not left us without guidance. In fact, He has given us a rule to follow that, when properly applied, can guide and govern our thoughts, speech and actions; however, just because we strive to practice this rule doesn't mean that others will do likewise. In other words, Jesus didn't say, "If you do unto others what you want them to do to you, they will treat you the same way." There is no guarantee that others will treat you the way you treat them, but the Golden Rule is not contingent upon how others behave. We have to obey it and practice it in spite of how others might respond. When we do, this one simple rule will change our lives, improve our relationships and ultimately equip us to make better decisions.

Discussion Questions

1. What is the Golden Rule? Why do you think we commonly call Matthew 7:12 the Golden Rule?

2. Is following the Golden Rule simple?

3. How can applying this one rule change your life and society as well?

4. Evangelistically speaking, how would this rule guide you in teaching the lost?

5. What makes applying the Golden Rule toward those who don't practice it difficult?

Chapter 9

The Power of Prayer
Prayer-Saturated Decisions

When I was in high school, basketball was my overwhelming obsession. The highlight of every summer was attending the Pocono Invitational Basketball Camp. I went every summer, and it was not unusual for me to spend four or five weeks at that camp. At the beginning of each week, players were evaluated and placed on a team they would practice and play with for the entire session. At the end of the week, the coach of each team prepared a report card for every player he coached during the week. I still have every one of those report cards. My favorite was from a coach who highlighted a few of my strengths, encouraged me to work on several of my weaknesses and then ended the evaluation with these three words: PRACTICE! PRACTICE! PRACTICE! He was telling me that the only way to maximize my strengths and improve upon my weaknesses was to practice as much as possible.

If you are serious about becoming a more faithful Christian by making better decisions, I have three words of advice for you: PRAY! PRAY! PRAY! This is the best advice I can offer. Saturate your life with prayer. Let prayer soak down into every corner of your daily calendar. In Psalm 55, King David said, "Evening and morning and at noon I will pray, and cry aloud, and He shall hear my voice" (v. 17). Every Christian should imitate David's example. In fact, there is an old song that encourages us to "whisper a prayer in the morning, whisper a prayer at noon; whisper a prayer in the evening, to keep your heart in tune."

There is no better way to keep your heart in tune with God than to bathe every decision in prayer. Think about how different your life would be if you actually spent one "sweet hour of prayer" with God each and every day. Sadly God gets much less than that from many of His children. Some are content to utter a few words of praise before they drift off to sleep while others never bother to talk to God at all – that is, until they are confronted with an emergency, and then they seldom know what to say.

Joseph Scriven was right to remind us that we have a friend in Jesus and that it is truly a privilege to carry everything to God in prayer. The most revealing phrase in his beloved hymn "What a Friend We Have in Jesus," though, forces us to admit to ourselves, "O what peace we often forfeit, O what needless pain we bear, All because we do not carry Everything to God in prayer." Throughout the remainder of this chapter, I would like to identify some of the blessings we forfeit and the pain we bear when we fail to spend sufficient time alone with God in prayer.

The Blessing of Wisdom

We should pray more because we all need the wisdom that comes from above. We live in confusing times. We are faced with many choices and decisions, and we don't always know what to do. There are young people trying to navigate through a culture that is changing at the speed of light. They are confronted with all of the same decisions teenagers have always had to make but with less certainty than what their parents and grandparents seemed to enjoy. They have to make important moral, social, political and religious decisions, and some of them feel completely overwhelmed by the challenge.

Quite frankly, it isn't much easier for adults. Those who are married carry a great deal of responsibility for their spouse and children. They have to make decisions that affect their families financially, emotionally and spiritually. It is a daunting task. Then there are those who lead God's people. They bear great responsibility. They are called to keep watch as men who will one day have to give an account. No wonder most of the public prayers offered on their behalf include some mention of the difficult decisions they have to make.

How are our children supposed to maneuver through the mine-field of adolescence and make it to adulthood as healthy, faithful and well-adjusted Christians? How are Christian adults supposed to lead their families and God's church in a generation that seems to have lost its moral and spiritual equilibrium? Where do we turn to find the wisdom to live for God in such chaotic and confusing times? The book of James holds the answer:

> If any of you lacks wisdom, let him ask of God, who gives to all liberally and without reproach, and it will be given to him. But let him ask in faith, with no doubting, for he who doubts is like a wave of the sea driven and tossed by the wind. For let not that man suppose that he will receive anything from the Lord; he is a double-minded man, unstable in all his ways. (James 1:5-8)

One of the major blessings we forfeit when we fail to saturate our lives with prayer is the blessing of God's divine wisdom. Would you pray more if you knew that prayer was the answer to all your confusion and that God would give you wisdom "liberally and without reproach"? When you look at it from that perspective, it is hard to understand why any of us would go through a single day without praying to God. We all need to pray more, and when we do, God will bless us with the wisdom we need to live for Him.

The Struggles of Temptation

We should pray more because we all face a daily battle with temptation. When Jesus taught His disciples how to pray, He taught them to make this request: "And do not lead us into temptation but deliver us from the evil one" (Matthew 6:13). I have a sneaking suspicion that many of us have not prayed that prayer and that we do not fight very hard or very long before giving into temptation. I suspect plenty of Christians never resist temptation because they find it much easier and more enjoyable to surrender to it. This is an ugly accusation, but I am afraid some believers do not want to be delivered from temptation; they want to be delivered from the threat of punishment. Because that is the case, they do whatever they are tempted to do and then ask God to forgive them at some point after they have sinned.

I want to suggest a better approach. Instead of the all too common pattern of temptation, followed by sin, followed by guilt, followed by shame, followed by prayer for God's forgiveness; why not break that cycle? Why not change to a different pattern that looks more like this – temptation, followed by prayer for God's strength, followed by resistance to sin and obedience to God's will resulting in praise and thanksgiving?

In the familiar words of Scriven's hymn, "Have we trials and temptations, is there trouble anywhere? We should never be discouraged; take it to the Lord in prayer!" In another song, written by Annie Hawks, we sing, "I need Thee every hour: Stay Thou near by; Temptations lose their pow'r When Thou art nigh" ("I Need Thee Every Hour"). If it is true that temptations lose their power when God is near, then we need to cultivate a spirit of nearness, and nothing contributes to deeper communion with God than prayer. The reason we fail so miserably in our battle with temptation is because we wait too long to pray. Many of us already know our weaknesses. We know our spiritual deficiencies, and we need to be praying about those things. We need to ask God for the wisdom to avoid temptation and the strength to resist it.

When we pray, God hears and God acts. Prayer gives us access to the very real power of God, and God, not prayer, helps us to conquer temptation. He enables us to overcome the lust of the eye, the lust of the flesh and the boastful pride of life. When is the last time you talked to God? Why don't you set this book aside for a few minutes, get down on your knees and pray to the One who made this promise, "Call upon Me in the day of trouble; I will deliver you, and you shall glorify Me" (Psalm 50:15).

The Reality of Trials

We should pray more because trials are part of the inescapable reality of life in a fallen world. I am amused and a little insulted by the prosperity gospel that suggests children of God will always be happy and never sad; they will always be healthy and never sick; and they will always be rich and never poor. It makes me wonder if the people who preach that gospel have ever read the book of Job or the rest of the Bible for that matter. Jesus always told His disciples the truth; He was always honest about the difficulties of discipleship. In John 16:33, He warned them saying, "In the world you will have tribulation." When Paul and Barnabas returned to Lystra, Iconium and Antioch "strengthening the souls of the disciples" and "exhorting them to continue in the faith" they reminded those new converts, "We must through many tribulations enter the kingdom of God" (Acts 14:21-22).

Christianity does not shelter us from the harsh realities of sickness, suffering and death. The painful truth about life is that life is full of pain. Most of us are in one of three stages in life. We are either entering into a trial, we are currently in the midst of a trial, or we are finally moving out of some painful ordeal. Trials are an unpleasant and undeniable part of this life, and we should not expect to endure them successfully without prayer. I want to encourage you to fix your eyes on Jesus because there is so much we can learn from His example.

When Jesus came to the Garden of Gethsemane, He told His disciples, "My soul is exceedingly sorrowful, even to death" (Matthew 26:38). The end of His life was drawing near and He knew it. Jesus was more familiar with messianic prophecy than most of us, and He knew what was going to happen to Him. He was going to be falsely accused, arrested and taken by force. He was going to be betrayed, deserted and denied. He was going to be beaten and spat upon. He was going to be tried and unjustly judged. He was going to hear His countrymen cry out for His life and for His blood. He was going to be mocked, flogged, crowned with thorns and crucified. He was going to be forsaken by the One whose fellowship He had never been without.

How was He able to endure such unthinkable trials? He prayed. Not once. Not twice, but three times. In fact, the writer of Hebrews tells us that "during the days of Jesus' life on earth, he offered up prayers and petitions with loud cries and tears to the one who could save him from death" (Hebrews 5:7 NIV84). Jesus prayed so intensely that "His sweat became like great drops of blood falling to the ground"

(Luke 22:44). Jesus prayed for the cup of His suffering to be taken away, but He also prayed if it could not be taken away unless He drank it, that God's will might be done (Matthew 26:39, 42).

What does Jesus teach us by His example? He teaches us that prayer is not always about getting what we want or getting out of the pain that sometimes comes along with doing God's will. Prayer is about preparing ourselves to do what God wants even when such obedience subjects us to painful trials instead of delivering us from them. Jesus prayed during the darkest hour of His life. Prayer empowered Jesus to endure the cross. Prayer can help us too.

The Need for Comfort, Mercy and Grace

We should pray more because there will be times when all of us need comfort, mercy and grace. We always need God. There are just times in life when we are more aware of that need. In nearly 20 years of ministry, I have had the privilege of serving people in some dark and painful moments. There was a week, just recently, when three of our members were diagnosed with terminal cancer. I received calls on Monday, Tuesday and Thursday with the devastating news. Each of those three people needed God, and they knew it.

I have been with husbands who have lost their wives and wives who have lost their husbands. I remember one time when I rushed to the home of one of our families who had just lost their 4-year-old daughter to cancer. When I walked into their living room, that mother was still holding the lifeless body of her sweet little girl. I felt like I was intruding on holy ground. I remember a 13-year-old boy hit by a car while riding his bike to school, and I remember walking into the hospital waiting room to comfort and cry with his parents. All of those people needed God; none of them doubted it.

What a joy and relief to open the Bible and discover that the Creator of all things is not distant, aloof or unconcerned. The God of Creation introduces himself to us as "the Father of mercies and the God of all comfort" (2 Corinthians 1:3), and He promises to be "near to those who have a broken heart" (Psalm 34:18). The psalmist reminds us that "God is our refuge and strength, a very present help in trouble" (46:1). I cannot think of a passage that offers more hope to hurting people or one that should inspire a greater appreciation for prayer than the words of Hebrews 4:

> Seeing then that we have a great High Priest who has passed through the heavens, Jesus the Son of God, let us hold fast our confession. For we do not have a High Priest who cannot sympathize with our weaknesses, but was in all points tempted as we are, yet without sin. Let us therefore come boldly to the throne of grace, that we may obtain mercy and find grace to help in time of need. (Hebrews 4:14-16)

Here is the truth about prayer. Too many of us pray because we want something from God. We want a happier life, a stronger faith, a healthier body, a more fulfilling marriage, a bigger bank account, a nicer car, a better job. If we are not careful our prayer list can look like a child's letter to Santa Claus. Tragedy has a way of stripping away our selfishness. There comes a point in life when we no longer want anything from God. We just want God, and the book of Hebrews says we can have Him because our great High Priest has made it possible for us to approach the throne of grace. When the tragedies that happen only to other people inevitably happen to us, we can go to God and obtain mercy. When the things we have hoped would never happen actually do happen, then we can "find grace to help in time of need."

We always need God. There are just moments when we are more painfully aware of that need. When those moments come, the best decision you can make is to run to the throne room of God's grace. The father of mercies and the God of all comfort will meet you there.

The Prayer of the Righteous

This chapter about prayer and the importance of saturating your life with prayer would seem somewhat incomplete if we concluded without taking just a little time to consider what James had to say about this subject. Near the end of the final chapter of his brief letter, James wrote these challenging and encouraging words:

> Is anyone among you suffering? Let him pray. Is anyone cheerful? Let him sing psalms. Is anyone among you sick? Let him call for the elders of the church, and let them pray over him, anointing him with oil in the name of the Lord. And the prayer of faith will save the sick, and the Lord will raise him up. And if he has committed sins, he will be forgiven. Confess your trespasses to one another, and pray for one another, that you may be healed. The effective, fervent prayer of a righteous man avails much. Elijah was a man with a nature like ours, and he prayed earnestly that it would not rain; and it did not rain on the land for three years and six months. And he prayed again, and the heaven gave rain, and the earth produced its fruit. (James 5:13-18)

There is so much about this passage that deserves closer consideration. James tells us that the prayers of a righteous person are powerful and effective. He reminds us that no matter what is happening in our lives, prayer is always a good idea. We can pray when the sun is shining and we can pray when the storm clouds are gathering. He reminds us of the importance of praying for those who are sick and the strength that comes from confessing our sins and praying for each other. But one of the most important things that James wrote in those few short verses is that "Elijah was a man with a nature like ours."

When Elijah prayed, God listened to him despite the fact that he was just a man with a nature like ours. He was just like us physically, emotionally and spiritually. Yet when he prayed, it didn't rain for three and a half years, and when he prayed again, it rained. If God answered his prayers, then God will answer ours too. One of the greatest failures of modern Christianity is the failure to pray. Prayer can help you to make life-changing decisions but first you have to make the life-changing decision to pray. I don't know a better way to end this chapter than with the question that comes from another of our great old hymns, "Ere you left your room this morning, did you think to pray?" ("Did You Think to Pray?" Mary A. Pepper Kidder).

Discussion Questions

1. What difference would a life of prayer make when you have major life decisions?

2. Compare Psalm 55:17 to 1 Thessalonians 5:17. How does this compare with your prayer life?

3. What truth is there to this saying: "God always answers prayers one of three ways – yes, no or later."

4. Jesus provides us with two great examples of prayer in the Gospels: the Lord's prayer (Matthew 6:9-13; Luke 11:2-4) and the prayer in the garden (Matthew 26:36-46; Luke 22:39-46). If we are to imitate Christ, how are we to pray based on His examples?

5. There is more to praying than supplication. What other elements should we include in our prayers?

Chapter 10

Ambassadors for Christ

Influence-Guarding Decisions

When my Dad was restored and the rest of my family was converted, many things changed instantly. Some habits, however, were deeply ingrained and took more time to overcome. The thing that lingered the longest was my ongoing struggle with inappropriate language. Some of my vocabulary was picked up at home; some of it was learned at school or from music, movies and television. Needless to say, I developed some bad habits that were not easy to change.

I played two years of basketball at Oklahoma Christian. I was a junior college transfer and a walk-on. Coach Dan Hays got me a work study job doing team laundry. I was at the bottom of the depth chart, but I was on the team and got to play with the best players on campus every day. One of the challenges of my position was guarding the starting point guard during daily scrimmages. It was a frustrating assignment because he was such a good player. Many times, my frustration boiled over, and it was not uncommon for me to whisper a few "choice" words under my breath. I assumed no one else could hear what I was saying.

During my two years on campus, my faith began to grow. I had great Bible professors and was listening to some of the best preaching I had ever heard. During that time, my focus shifted from basketball. As soon as I finished my education degree, I enrolled in the ministry program and began preparing for a life of Christian service. As I grew in faith, I decided the time had come to start sharing the gospel with my friends. The starting point guard, the guy I was competing against every day in practice, seemed like an obvious prospect for evangelism. I remember catching him outside the locker room and awkwardly trying to begin a spiritual conversation.

It did not take him long to cut me off. I don't remember his exact words, but he said something to this effect, "Tim, you guard me every day in practice, and I hear the way you talk. Why should I listen to anything you have to say about religion?" His pointed remarks brought our brief conversation to an abrupt conclusion. That failed attempt to share the gospel remains one of the most embarrassing moments of my life, but it taught me an important lesson. If people do not respect our example, they will not listen to our saving message. I failed to guard my influence, and that decision not only resulted in personal embarrassment but also caused my friend to miss a crucial opportunity. To my knowledge, he has never obeyed the gospel.

In his book, *The Gravedigger File*, author Os Guinness made the following charge against modern Christians, "It's not that they aren't where they should be, but that they aren't what they should be where they are" (79-80). If that charge is true, and it certainly was in my case, how do we become what we are supposed be? How do we maximize our opportunities to influence the world for Christ? At least five biblical metaphors teach us how to be people of influence. A brief look at each one should help us to make influence-guarding decisions.

The Salt of the Earth

The first metaphor is found in Matthew 5:13 when Jesus told His disciples, "You are the salt of the earth; but if the salt loses its flavor, how shall it be seasoned? It is then good for nothing but to be thrown out and trampled underfoot by men." Salt is influential. It is conspicuous by its presence. My grandmother used to bake homemade pies, and her apple pie was my favorite. I used to take a slice of that pie, put it in a bowl with just a little milk and then sprinkle sugar on top. One time, I reached into the wrong canister and accidentally sprinkled salt on my pie instead of sugar. The salt was conspicuous by its presence. I noticed the difference after one bite; but salt is also conspicuous by its absence. Try to imagine how hard it would be to choke down a serving of mashed potatoes without salt. It is not a very appetizing thought.

Salt does a lot of things. It was used as a preservative in the first century. It purifies and adds flavor, but salt also creates thirst. It is nearly impossible to eat a bag of chips or to munch on a bowl of popcorn without having something to drink. Salt makes you thirsty. The same thing should be said about Christian influence. There should be something about the way we live for Jesus that causes other people to thirst for Him.

I already mentioned a two-year period at Oklahoma Christian that really impacted my faith. That was when I first met Avon Malone. He was part of the Bible faculty and preached for the Wilshire congregation in Oklahoma City. I would be hard-pressed to exaggerate his profound influence on my life. His reverence for Scripture and his dedication to the inspired text motivated me to grow in my own love for God's Word and contributed greatly to my decision to enter the ministry.

Shortly after I moved to Mount Vernon, Mo., to begin my first full-time work, Avon agreed to hold a gospel meeting for the congregation there. I remember sitting next to him during communion. As prayers were being offered and trays were being passed, I looked over at my mentor and saw tears streaming down his cheeks; he was weeping. Avon loved Jesus so much. That kind of passion for the Lord is extremely contagious; it makes other people hunger and thirst for Him.

The Light of the World

How are we supposed to influence the world for Christ? The second metaphor is found in the same context as the first. Listen to what else Jesus had to say in Matthew 5:

> You are the light of the world. A city that is set on a hill cannot be hidden. Nor do they light a lamp and put it under a basket, but on a lampstand, and it gives light to all who are in the house. Let your light so shine before men, that they may see your good works and glorify your Father in heaven. (vv. 14-16)

As Christians, we are the light of the world. Jesus does not want us to hide our light under a basket. He wants us to put it on a stand. In the words of Paul, the Lord expects those who follow Him to "shine as lights in the world" (Philippians 2:15). That, after all, is exactly what Jesus did. According to the prophet Isaiah, when Jesus came into the world "people who sat in darkness" saw "a great light" (Isaiah 9:1-2; Matthew 4:16). Through His teaching and through the example of His perfect life, Jesus brought light to a region of the world that had previously been swallowed up by darkness. That is exactly what He wants His followers to do.

A few years ago, I sat in the audience and listened as Ralph Burcham told the fascinating story of his missionary efforts in the war-torn country of Vietnam. When Ralph and his wife, Gladys, made the decision to serve God in Vietnam, they had two small children and no guarantee they or their children would be safe. They understood by going to the mission field they were putting themselves in harm's way. A local newspaper reporter somehow found out about their plans. During an interview the night before they left the country, he asked Ralph, "What if you don't return?" I will never forget what he told that reporter: "We don't have to return. We just have to go." Ralph and Gladys understood that the light of Christian influence is needed in dark places.

As a convert to Christianity, I still remember the darkness of life without God, without Jesus, without the influence of the Bible and the loving encouragement of the church. Not only can I remember the darkness, I distinctly remember when the light of Christian influence came into my life and illuminated everything. It reminds me of a monument erected in honor of a South Pacific missionary. The monument simply said, "When he came there was no light. When he left there was no darkness." That's a perfect description of my conversion, but it is also a powerful reminder of our mission in the world. God has called us to be salt and light.

The Leaven That Increases

How are we supposed to influence the world for Christ? Jesus used many parables to explain what the kingdom of God was like.

In one of those parables Jesus said, "To what shall I liken the kingdom of God? It is like leaven, which a woman took and hid in three measures of meal till it was all leavened" (Luke 13:20-21). This is the third metaphor. Our influence, much like the leaven in our Lord's parable, should permeate every relationship we have. That is the pervasive nature of our faith; it affects everything it touches. It is contagious and aggressive. If you are a Christian, the godly influence that comes from your faith should not be something you have to cultivate nor should anyone have to coerce you into exerting it. Leaven does what it does because of what it is; in other words, if you are leaven you will leaven.

I was working on a sermon one Saturday afternoon when the phone rang. The person calling was not a Christian. He called to ask questions about the church of Christ because he was dating a girl who had been raised in the church. It is hard to know what motivated that first contact. Early on I believed he was just looking for enough information to argue effectively with his girlfriend, but something unexpected happened. They actually visited one of our services. He eventually expressed interest in a personal Bible study and ended up being baptized into Christ. Not long after his conversion, he enrolled in a preacher-training school and over a three-year period not only completed his training but also succeeded in leading his sister, mother, father, niece and a family friend to Christ.

Another young man started playing basketball in our gym. That was his first contact with our congregation, but he eventually stopped coming just to play basketball and started attending worship services and Bible classes as well. Before too long, he made the good confession and put on Christ in baptism. Not long after his conversion, that young man told me, "After I stopped coming in that door (he was pointing to the gym) and started coming in this door (he then pointed to the main entrance to our auditorium), my whole life began to change."

His life really did change, and he didn't keep those positive changes to himself. In less than two years, this new convert has been instrumental in leading three of his friends and one of his sisters to faith in Christ. You see, God never intended for us to be a reservoir for

His blessings; He wants us to be a channel. In other words, as God pours His blessings into our lives, He wants them not only to flow to us but also to flow through us so that others can know the joy of salvation. If you are leaven, you will leaven!

An Epistle of Christ

How are we supposed to influence the world for Christ? The next metaphor comes from the inspired pen of Paul. In his second letter to the church in Corinth, he wrote these words, "You are our epistle written in our hearts, known and read by all men; clearly you are an epistle of Christ, ministered by us, written not with ink but by the Spirit of the living God, not on tablets of stone but on tablets of flesh, that is, of the heart" (2 Corinthians 3:2-3). The word "epistle" basically means a letter, and Paul emphasizes that we are to be "known and read by all men."

Think about the implications of that phrase. If your life is an open book, what does it say to others about Jesus? As people read the pages of your life what do they learn about you? More importantly, what impact does that have on how they see Jesus and the church? Several years ago, I read an article about Colt McCoy who was the starting quarterback for a major college football program. He was a faithful member of the Lord's church and a very gifted young athlete. Apparently, the day after a difficult loss, in a game in which McCoy suffered a painful injury, his father received an unexpected phone call. The caller said something to this effect:

> I have got to tell you I've never seen anything like your son. I was sitting in church this morning when he walked in. He was a little late, but he was there. He was all beat up, but he was there. I know that he couldn't have gotten home before three or four in the morning and he must have been tired, but he was there for our 9:00 a.m. service … and my little boy saw that. That was the biggest impression anyone has ever made on my 10-year-old son! (King, "The Real McCoy," Paraphrased)

Actions really do speak louder than words. When we take on

the name of Jesus and claim to be Christians like the ones you read about in the Bible, people have every right to expect us to live by a higher standard. They deserve to see commitment and consistency as we live out our faith. If we truly are "known and read by all men," what others know about us and what they hear us say and see us do is of utmost importance.

Ambassadors for Christ

How are we supposed to influence the world for Christ? The fifth and final metaphor is also found in Paul's second letter to the Corinthians. After reminding the Christians in Corinth that they should live for the One who died for them, Paul wrote these memorable words:

> Now all things are of God, who has reconciled us to Himself through Jesus Christ, and has given us the ministry of reconciliation, that is, that God was in Christ reconciling the world to Himself, not imputing their trespasses to them, and has committed to us the word of reconciliation. Now then, we are ambassadors for Christ, as though God were pleading through us: we implore you on Christ's behalf, be reconciled to God. (2 Corinthians 5:18-20)

Many writers and preachers have reached the conclusion that only the apostles enjoyed the privilege of being recognized as ambassadors for Christ. Although that might be true in the most technical sense, I don't see how sincere Christians could see themselves as anything other than goodwill ambassadors for Jesus. This is a big responsibility because whatever people tend to think about you is most likely what they are going to think about every other Christian they meet. When you become a Christian, your reputation becomes "our" reputation. Consider just a few examples.

If you are Canadian and you have an unpleasant encounter with an American, you might be tempted to think all Americans are like the one unpleasant American you encountered. Or if you are an American and you have a disagreeable encounter with someone of middle-eastern descent, you might very well conclude that everyone from that region of the world is like the one disagreeable person you had the misfortune to meet. This tendency is not limited to nationality; it can also be applied to different races. If you are black and you have a negative interaction with a white person, that negative interaction might impact how you see all white people, and if you are white and you have just one negative interaction with a black person that negative interaction might affect how you see all black people. My primary concern is not with nationality or race; my primary concern is spiritual and religious in nature.

If you are a judgmental, hypocritical and mean-spirited Christian, there is a very good possibility that people will conclude that whatever is true about you must also be true about every other Christian and about the church in general. However, if you are loving, kind and helpful, those who meet you will most likely develop a positive perception of Christianity and the Lord's church based on the favorable impression left by your faith and conduct.

When it comes to influence, it is nearly impossible to be neutral. Your influence can be someone's best reason for following Jesus or their biggest excuse for rejecting Him. One word or one act could open the door to salvation; one word or one act could also close that door forever. That's why you need to guard your influence by consistently choosing right over wrong and God's best over the merely good enough. Decisions really are important!

Discussion Questions

1. Define metaphor. List the five biblical metaphors used in this chapter.

2. Paul said, "We are ambassadors for Christ." What does an ambassador for our nation do for our country? What does Paul say Christian ambassadors should do?

3. What properties of salt and light should we as Christians uphold?

4. Name some ways our influence should permeate our relationships.

5. How are we known and read by all men?

Chapter 11

Whatever You Think
Thought-Purifying Decisions

"**N**on-Conformist!" That word was emblazoned in big black letters across the back of his T-shirt and right below that bold one-word statement was this familiar passage of Scripture, "And do not be conformed to this world, but be transformed by the renewing of your mind, that you may prove what is that good and acceptable and perfect will of God" (Romans 12:2). Ironically, the teenage boy who was wearing that T-shirt had just purchased a ticket to watch a movie that included graphic violence, vulgar language and inappropriate sexual content. The poor kid was a walking, talking contradiction. He claimed to be the kind of Christian who is not pressed into the image of this world, but at the same time he was filling his eyes, ears and thoughts with the world's value system.

Many Christians, like the young man I encountered at the movie theater, are making the same mistake because they fail to see the connection between their thoughts and their actions. They stubbornly insist that what they look at, listen to, watch and read has little or no impact on their faith, but the Word of God tells a different story. In fact, Paul explained it this way in Galatians 6:7: "Do not be deceived, God is not mocked; for whatever a man sows that he will also reap." The law of sowing and reaping has spiritual consequences that cannot be denied or ignored. Mel Weldon's brief poem offers this practical reminder:

My mind is a garden. My thoughts are the seeds.
My harvest will be either flowers or weeds.

Removing the Bad

If you are tired of growing weeds and you want to change your life by making different and better decisions, then it is essential to change the way you think because your thoughts make you what you are. According to Proverbs 23:7, "For as he thinks in his heart, so is he." Ralph Waldo Emerson put it this way, "A man is what he thinks about all day long," and the Roman Emperor Marcus Aurelius concluded that "our life is what our thoughts make it." Biblical evidence strongly supports that conclusion. Just six chapters into the story of the Bible, the Word of God gives the following assessment of man and his mindset: "Then the LORD saw that the wickedness of man was great in the earth, and that every intent of the thoughts of his heart was only evil continually" (Genesis 6:5). Further along the timeline of human history, the psalmist pointed out that "the wicked in his proud countenance does not seek God; God is in none of his thoughts" (Psalm 10:4).

These two verses accurately describe the way some people think. The content of their thought life could be summarized as "only evil all the time" and "never God any time." There are actually people who never think about God. They never think about God's existence. They never consider His justice, mercy and grace. They never think about God's creative power, His sustaining care or His redeeming love. The only thing they think about is evil all the time. The closing verses of Romans 1 reveal a disturbing description of how people live when God is crowded out of all their thoughts. According to Paul, such people are:

> filled with all unrighteousness, sexual immorality, wickedness, covetousness, maliciousness; full of envy, murder, strife, deceit, evil-mindedness; they are whisperers, backbiters, haters of God, violent, proud, boasters, inventors of evil things, disobedient to parents, undiscerning, untrustworthy, unloving, unforgiving, unmerciful; who, knowing the righteous judgment of God, that those who practice such things are deserving of death, not only do the same but also approve of those who practice them. (Romans 1:29-32)

What a tragic portrait of life without God! These people have been memorialized in Scripture and will always be remembered for their futile thoughts and foolish hearts (Romans 1:21). They became unrighteous, immoral, wicked and malicious because their thoughts were unrighteous, immoral, wicked and malicious. They refused to "retain God in their knowledge" and ended up doing things "which are not fitting" (v. 28). In the end, they sank to the level of their thoughts. You are not immune to the same possibility. Your thoughts make you who you are; therefore, "keep your heart with all diligence, for out of it spring the issues of life" (Proverbs 4:23).

Never underestimate the power and influence of your thoughts. There is an undeniable relationship between your thoughts and the decisions you make. The devil knows this and uses it to his advantage. Think about the very first sin. Why did Eve eat the forbidden fruit? When the serpent first approached Eve, her thinking was governed by God. She understood God's will concerning the tree in the middle of the garden, and she was able to explain exactly what God had said concerning the fruit of that tree. She told the serpent, "We may eat the fruit of the trees of the garden; but of the fruit of the tree which is in the midst of the garden, God has said, 'You shall not eat it, nor shall you touch it, lest you die'" (Genesis 3:2-3).

Before her unfortunate encounter with the serpent, Eve understood God's command. She was content to live within the limits of God's will; but the serpent was "cunning" (Genesis 3:1), and he knew that the only way to change Eve's behavior was to change her thinking. That is exactly what he set out to accomplish. He began by contradicting the direct command God had given Adam. God's original command was clear and concise, "The day that you eat of it you shall surely die" (2:17). The serpent, however, told Eve, "You will not surely die" (3:4). He only added one word to what God said, but it was enough to change the entire meaning of His command.

The serpent then proceeded to plant seeds of doubt and desire in Eve's mind with these deceptive words, "For God knows that in the day you eat of it your eyes will be opened, and you will be like God, knowing good and evil" (Genesis 3:5). After Eve's brief conversation with the serpent, she started to think differently about the "forbidden" fruit. She began to notice "that the tree was good for food" and "that it was pleasant to the eyes" and that it was "desirable to make one wise" (v. 6). A subtle shift in Eve's thought process resulted in a dramatic change in her behavior. "She took of its fruit and ate. She also gave to her husband with her, and he ate" (v. 6).

God wants you to learn an important lesson from this story. He wants you to understand that the mind is the primary battlefield for the soul. You can't lose the battle for your mind and win the battle for your soul. Eve sinned because she allowed the devil to change the way she thought about God, about God's command, about the tree of the knowledge of good and evil and its fruit. If you are serious about consistently making better decisions, then you have to guard your thoughts. Paul said it this way: "Casting down arguments and every high thing that exalts itself against the knowledge of God, bringing every thought into captivity to the obedience of Christ" (2 Corinthians 10:5).

This explains why many sincere Christians fail. They refuse to exert the spiritual energy needed to consistently expel sinful thoughts from their imagination. It is impossible to keep stray thoughts from floating through your mind, but you do not have to let them settle there. Be honest. There are times when you should turn off the radio, walk out of the movie theater, log off of the computer, put down the magazine, change the channel or excuse yourself from a conversation, but you linger longer than you should. A well-known children's song warns, "Be careful little eyes what you see," and "be careful little ears what you hear." We never reach a point in our lives where that song no longer applies.

Joshua famously declared, "Choose for yourselves this day whom you will serve … . But as for me and my house, we will serve the LORD" (Joshua 24:15). When it comes to the battle for the mind, you have to make the same decision Joshua made, but you have to make it over and over again every single day. In other words, you have to choose this day, every day, to serve the Lord by conquering sinful thoughts and bringing them into submission to the Lordship of Jesus Christ.

Exchange Bad for Good

It is not enough to remove bad thoughts; you must replace them with something good. The book of James provides a concise, one-verse summary of this concept. According to James, we must, "lay aside all filthiness and overflow of wickedness, and receive with meekness the implanted word, which is able to save your souls" (James 1:21). Before we can properly receive the saving word of God, we need to purify our hearts and our minds. We have to get rid of all the filthy and wicked thoughts that have taken residence within our imagination. Only then can we receive God's message of salvation. Jesus basically described the same concept in one of his many parables. According to Jesus:

> When an unclean spirit goes out of a man, he goes through dry places, seeking rest, and finds none. Then he says, "I will return to my house from which I came." And when he comes, he finds it empty, swept, and put in order. Then he goes and takes with him seven other spirits more wicked than himself, and they enter and dwell there; and the last state of that man is worse than the first. So shall it also be with this wicked generation. (Matthew 12:43-45)

The man in this parable got off to a great beginning. He clearly had good intentions. He swept his spiritual house and started to put things in order, but he did not fill it with good things. The Lord's story hinges on that crucial detail. When the evil spirit returned to the house from which he came, he found it empty. Jesus is comparing an empty house to an empty mind, and He is warning us that Satan thrives under such conditions. Jesus is warning us that it is not enough to evict the old tenant; we have to replace the old with something new. In other words, the only way to subtract bad habits permanently is to add good ones.

In another parable, Jesus said, "Hear Me, everyone, and understand: There is nothing that enters a man from outside which can defile him; but the things which come out of him, those are the things that defile a man" (Mark 7:14-15). As was the case on several other occasions,

His disciples were confused so they "asked Him concerning the parable" (v. 17). Jesus gave the following explanation:

> Then are you also without understanding? Do you not see that whatever goes into a person from outside cannot defile him, since it enters not his heart but his stomach, and is expelled? (Thus he declared all foods clean.) ... What comes out of a person is what defiles him. For from within, out of the heart of man, come evil thoughts, sexual immorality, theft, murder, adultery, coveting, wickedness, deceit, sensuality, envy, slander, pride, foolishness. All these evil things come from within, and they defile a person. (Mark 7:18-23 ESV)

If that is the case, and it is because Jesus said it is, then what does a person do when he or she has allowed "all these evil things" to enter and settle down into the heart? Once "evil thoughts" have entered your mind, how do you get them out? You have to displace them.

Cleaning House

I have never been comfortable using object lessons in my teaching, but I do remember one illustration that I used with some degree of effectiveness. I took a cup of cola, placed it in a large rubber tub and proceeded to pour a pitcher of water into the cup. I kept pouring more and more water into that cup until every last drop of the cola had been completely displaced. The imagery was memorable. I wanted my students to understand that the only way to change their thinking was to displace sinful thoughts with something more helpful. I'd like to conclude this chapter by suggesting four things you can do to replace evil thoughts with something good.

Read and Memorize

First, read and memorize Scripture. Because an empty mind will always be filled, be proactive. Build time into your daily schedule for reading God's Word, but don't just read God's Word – memorize it. That's what David did. Psalm 119 is a chapter that deals exclusively with the blessings and benefits of studying and obeying God's Word.

In verse 9 of that chapter King David asked this question, "How can a young man cleanse his way?" The answer was simple and direct, "By taking heed according to Your word." In verse 11, David went on to declare, "Your word I have hidden in my heart, that I might not sin against You!"

Jesus used this approach with great effectiveness. When the devil tempted Him, Jesus defended Himself with Scripture saying, "It is written" three times (Matthew 4:4, 7, 10). The same tactic can work for you, but don't just memorize random passages of Scripture. Look for verses that address your precise area of weakness. For instance, if you struggle with gossip, lust, pride, selfishness or greed, find passages from God's Word that deal with those specific sins. Memorize those passages and call upon them in your hour of need. You might even say them out loud for added emphasis.

Pray

Second, "pray without ceasing" (1 Thessalonians 5:17). Some men need to pray, and they don't know how. Others know how to pray, but they never do. Both classes of men are equally poor, the first from ignorance and the second from negligence. Never postpone prayer for errands or busy work. Nothing is more urgent than prayer. It is your most pressing obligation. Surrender to every inclination toward prayer.

Start every day in prayer. In Psalm 5, King David said, "Give ear to my words, O LORD, consider my meditation. Give heed to the voice of my cry, my King and my God, for to You I will pray. My voice You shall hear in the morning, O LORD; in the morning I will direct it to You, and I will look up" (vv. 1-3). David was the king of Israel. He must have carried many pressing responsibilities, but he had a standing appointment with God. He began each day in prayer. Regardless of whatever else might have been happening in his life, David made this promise, "My voice You shall hear in the morning, O LORD."

If you are struggling to keep your thoughts under God's control, the best thing you can do is to pray your way through the day. Look for windows of opportunity to squeeze prayer between everything else you are doing. Tell God how much you love Him. Ask Him for the help you need. Thank Him for all the wonderful things He has done. Confess your sins to Him. Plead for His forgiveness. Pray for others. Ask, seek and knock (Matthew 7:7). Pray and don't ever lose heart (Luke 18:1).

Sing

Third, sing and make melody in your heart to the Lord (Ephesians 5:19). When the ark of God was safely returned to the people of Israel, King David wrote a psalm to thank the Lord. As part of that psalm he wrote these words, "Sing to Him, sing psalms to Him; talk of all His wondrous works! ... Sing to the LORD, all the earth; proclaim the good news of His salvation from day to day" (1 Chronicles 16:9, 23). In Psalm 100, God's people were commanded to "make a joyful shout to the LORD" (v. 1) and "come before his presence with singing" (v. 2). They were also instructed to "enter into His gates with thanksgiving, and into His courts with praise" (v. 4).

Some people have a hard time expressing themselves. If you are one of those people, find a few songs that express what you have always wanted to say to God and sing those songs to Him. If you have to spend a lot of time driving to and from work or for work, make good use of that time. Fill your mind with a message of praise instead of listening to secular music or talk radio. Remember, it is not enough to get rid of sinful thoughts; you need to replace them with something positive and productive.

Fellowship

Fourth, spend time with good people. We all know that "evil company corrupts good habits" (1 Corinthians 15:33), but the opposite is also true. We can improve our thoughts and our behavior by spending time with faithful people. According to Proverbs 27:17, "As iron sharpens iron, so a man sharpens the countenance of his friend." Good people bring out the best in others; they "edify one another" (1 Thessalonians 5:11) and stir one another up to "love and good works" (Hebrews 10:24).

One of my favorite stories has always been the one about a little girl who passed away. Trying to determine what would be a fitting epitaph to put on her marker, her friends finally decided to inscribe this tribute, "It was easier to be good when she was around." If you are struggling with sinful thoughts, the worst thing you can do is befriend people who encourage your weaknesses. In the song, "Take Time to Be Holy," William D. Longstaff offered this advice: "Make friends of God's children." That's good advice because it really is easier to be good when the right people are around.

How do you permanently subtract bad habits? You have to add good ones. Read and memorize Scripture. Pray without ceasing. Sing and make melody in your heart to the Lord. Spend time with good people. I hope that you will not dismiss these simple suggestions. Remember, an empty mind will always be filled. You can fill it, or the devil will do it for you. There is no better way to conclude this chapter than with the memorable appeal Paul made to his beloved friends in the ancient city of Philippi:

> Finally, brethren, whatever things are true, whatever things are noble, whatever things are just, whatever things are pure, whatever things are lovely, whatever things are of good report, if there is any virtue and if there is anything praiseworthy – meditate on these things. (Philippians 4:8)

Discussion Questions

1. What is the meaning of Proverbs 23:7 when it says, "As a man thinks in his heart, so is he"?

2. Eve sinned because she allowed the devil to change her thoughts about God's command. How does the devil do this to us today?

3. What are some ways today's Christians could fill their minds with bad thoughts?

4. What are some strategies for replacing bad thoughts with good?

5. Read Philippians 4:8. How can meditating on the things Paul mentions help someone who is struggling with sinful thoughts?

Chapter 12

Heaven or Hell?
Eternity-Minded Decisions

"**K**eep eternity before the children." This was a young mother's dying request; the final instructions she left for her husband. There is a ring of urgency to her appeal along with an undeniable sense of spiritual priority. Some parents focus on their children's health, education, success and happiness. They are so consumed with the immediate that they give little or no thought to the eternal. It is a common mistake, but one the woman in this story refused to make. She clearly understood that "the things which are seen are temporary, but the things which are not seen are eternal" (2 Corinthians 4:18). She chose to focus on the unseen, eternal things of God.

This is a book about making decisions. Any book of this nature would be incomplete without making some effort to keep eternity before God's children. If decisions affect character, have inescapable consequences and determine destiny, how do you make better decisions? How do you consistently choose right over wrong and God's best over the merely "good enough"? You have to live in view of vast eternity. This is an appeal that men of God in past generations used to make in their preaching; it is also what I am urging readers of this book to do. Carefully consider the eternal consequences of your decisions. Make the concerted effort to live in view of vast eternity.

Considering eternity is difficult because we live in a generation that has given little thought to life after death. In fact, we have given so little consideration to eternity that many people have a hard time wrapping their minds around the concept. The math doesn't add up. The hymn "Amazing Grace" by John Newton includes this verse which was later added by Harriet Beecher Stowe in her book, *Uncle Tom's Cabin*:

> When we've been there ten thousand years,
> Bright, shining as the sun,
> We've no less days to sing God's praise
> Than when we first begun.

When you subtract 10,000 from eternity, you might expect to get 10,000 less than what you started with; but in the words of this hymn, "We've no less days to sing God's praise than when we first begun." What do you get when you subtract 10,000 from eternity? You still have eternity. It lasts forever and forever and forever. It never ends.

Creative efforts have been made to illustrate the vastness of eternity. Of the many illustrations I have read, two stand out as being the most memorable, impactful and convicting. The first one involves a massive cargo ship filled with little green peas. Every time the ship circumnavigates the globe you throw out one pea, then you sail around the world again and throw out another. The process is repeated over and over again until the great hold of the ship is finally empty. How long would it take to get down to the last little green pea? Regardless of the time required – that is still not eternity.

The second illustration begins with an ant walking around the equator. By passing over the same terrain repetitively, the ant first creates a path and then the path, over the course of many years, eventually becomes a trench. How much time would it take for that little ant to dig a trench so deep that the earth finally split in half? If such a thing were possible, it would require a mind-boggling amount of time – but that is still not eternity.

Eternity is forever, and according to Jesus, every person who has ever lived is going to spend eternity in one of two places. They are either going to "go away into everlasting punishment" or they are going to enter "into eternal life" (Matthew 25:46). There is no middle ground for those who are too good for hell but not quite good enough for heaven. There is no third alternative. Responsible people should, therefore, seek to learn as much as they can about these two places so as to make the best possible decision about their eternal destiny.

Hell: A Place of Torment

Let's start by taking a closer look at hell. What is hell like? One of the best biblical descriptions is recorded in Luke 16. The Lord's parable about the rich man and Lazarus describes the Hadean realm, which is understood to be an intermediary stop between death and judgment, but this story still gives us an accurate picture of what it will be like to be lost. It is not a pretty picture. According to Jesus:

> There was a certain rich man who was clothed in purple and fine linen and fared sumptuously every day. But there was a certain beggar named Lazarus, full of sores, who was laid at his gate, desiring to be fed with the crumbs which fell from the rich man's table. Moreover the dogs came and licked his sores. So it was that the beggar died, and was carried by the angels to Abraham's bosom. The rich man also died and was buried. And being in torments in Hades, he lifted up his eyes and saw Abraham afar off, and Lazarus in his bosom. Then he cried and said, "Father Abraham, have mercy on me, and send Lazarus that he may dip the tip of his finger in water and cool my tongue; for I am tormented in this flame." But Abraham said, "Son, remember that in your lifetime you received your good things, and likewise Lazarus evil things; but now he is comforted and you are tormented. And besides all this, between us and you there is a great gulf fixed, so that those who want to pass from here to you cannot, nor can those from there pass to us." Then he said, "I beg you therefore, father, that you would send him to my father's house, for I have five brothers, that he may testify to them, lest they also come to this place of torment." (Luke 16:19-28)

We learn three things about hell from Jesus' parable. First of all, we learn that hell is a place of punishment. Some form of the word "torment" is used four times to describe the rich man's agony, and he testified in his own words, "I am tormented in this flame" (Luke 16:24). The Bible contains many graphic descriptions of hell; the majority of them make unsettling references to fire. Hell is described as "the lake of fire" (Revelation 20:15), "the lake which burns with fire and brimstone" (21:8), "the everlasting fire" (Matthew 25:41), "the fire that shall never be quenched" (Mark 9:43) and "the vengeance of eternal fire" (Jude 7).

Along with all these references to the flames of hell, we also have passages that tell us it is a place of "outer darkness" where "there will be weeping and gnashing of teeth" (Matthew 8:12) and where people "will be tormented day and night forever and ever" (Revelation 20:10). According to the Bible, hell is a place of endless punishment.

God's Word also makes it clear that there will be no relief and no escape. When the rich man asked Abraham to have Lazarus cool his tongue with a drop of water, Abraham made it clear that such a request could not be granted; in fact, he said, "Between us and you there is a great gulf fixed, so that those who want to pass from here to you cannot, nor can those from there pass to us" (Luke 16:26). Even if Abraham had wanted to grant the rich man's request, he couldn't do it because of the great gulf that separated them. Hell is a place of eternal punishment. There is no relief. There is no escape. There is no end. As I said, it is not a very pretty picture, but we haven't even mentioned the worst part about being lost in hell.

The worst thing about hell is that God will not be there. As he was describing those who did not know God and had not obeyed the gospel, Paul told the Thessalonians, "These shall be punished with everlasting destruction from the presence of the Lord and from the glory of His power" (2 Thessalonians 1:9). Not only does Paul restate what we already learned about everlasting punishment; he also explains that the punishment includes the eternal loss of God's presence. It really is a "terrible tho't, to cry 'too late' – 'Jesus, I come to Thee.' "

Heaven: A Place of Joy

Let's shift our attention to happier thoughts. What is heaven like? Heaven and hell are polar opposites. Hell is a place of unimaginable pain and agony. Heaven is a place of indescribable comfort and joy. How do you try to describe the indescribable beauty of heaven? John gives us a most appealing and encouraging description of heaven in Revelation 21:

Now I saw a new heaven and a new earth, for the first heaven and the first earth had passed away. Also there was no more sea. Then I, John, saw the holy city, New Jerusalem, coming down out of heaven from God, prepared as a bride adorned for her husband. And I heard a loud voice from heaven saying, "Behold, the tabernacle of God is with men, and He will dwell with them, and they shall be His people. God Himself will be with them and be their God. And God will wipe away every tear from their eyes; there shall be no more death, nor sorrow, nor crying. There shall be no more pain, for the former things have passed away." (Revelation 21:1-4)

What makes heaven such a wonderful place? Four things will not be there. According to John's revelation, there will be no more pain in heaven. Wouldn't it be great to be in a place with no more pain? There is so much suffering in the world. People live with chronic pain and never get any relief from their constant agony. Others suffer from the emotional pain that comes from grief, abuse or loneliness, and then there is also a spiritual pain much harder to describe. It is the pain of sin and all that has been lost because of it. In heaven, there will be no more pain.

There will be no more sorrow. One of the great blessings of ministry is that you are invited into the most important moments in people's lives. When a baby is born or when someone graduates or when a young couple marries, they want you there; and when a loved one dies or a baby is delivered stillborn or when the diagnosis is cancer or a spouse is guilty of the worst kind of unfaithfulness, the people you minister to want you there. Pain and sorrow go hand in hand. They are an undeniable part of life here and now; but in heaven there will be no more pain. In heaven, there will be no more sorrow.

"He's gone." I still remember the pain in her voice when my wife called me at camp to tell me the news. Her granddaddy was like a father figure to her. It was devastating; death always is. Paul told the saints in Thessalonica, that Christians do not "sorrow as others who have no hope" (2 Thessalonians 4:13). Some people are under the mistaken impression that Christians don't grieve. After all, we believe in Jesus, we trust in His promises and we look forward to a home in heaven; why grieve? But God's Word never says that Christian people shouldn't grieve. It simply says that we do not grieve like those who have no hope. Physical death is the separation of man's spirit from his body (James 2:26), but it is also the separation of man from those who know and love him best. That hurts, terribly. In heaven, there will be no more separation. There will be no more death.

Think about that inspired picture. No more pain. No more sorrow. No more death. Doesn't that explain why there will be no more crying in heaven? "God will wipe away every tear" (Revelation 21:4). That is such a sweet and tender picture of God. I love the imagery. My son is a tough little boy; but sometimes when he plays too hard or tries something too adventurous he hurts himself. When he cries, he has the biggest tears. He usually goes to his mother for comfort, but on the rare occasions that he comes to me with his pain I take him in my arms and wipe the tears from his eyes.

That's what God is going to do for us when we get to heaven. He is going to destroy death. He is going to take away pain and sorrow. He is going to wipe the tears from our eyes, and He will put an end to our crying forevermore. But one more thing about heaven makes it such a special place. God will be there.

John tells us that "the tabernacle of God is with men, and He will dwell with them ... God Himself will be with them and be their God" (Revelation 21:3). When I was a little boy, I used to wonder if there would be basketball in heaven. That sounds silly and immature now, but as a little boy I didn't think it would be possible for me to be happy in a place that didn't have basketball. From a more mature perspective, I am just content to know God will be there. Heaven will still be heaven without basketball; but heaven would not be heaven without God. The best part about heaven is that God will be there.

In the first of his three letters, John made this remarkable promise, when he said that "we shall see Him as He is" and "we shall be like Him" (1 John 3:2). What an incredible moment that is going to be.

Most of the people who invest time reading a book like this have been studying about, singing about and praying to God for years. When you finally get to heaven, you are going to see Him. You are going to see the One who spoke the world into existence. You are going to see the One who so loved the world that He gave His only Son. You are going to see Him and you are going to be like Him. The worst thing about hell is that God won't be there. The best thing about heaven is that God will be our God. We are going to see Him, and He is going to live with us forever.

More than 20 years ago, the Salt Lake Valley Church of Christ hired me to serve as their summer youth intern. I arrived in Utah just as school was letting out for the summer. Because I was there to work with young people and their families, it seemed appropriate for me to attend the graduation ceremonies taking place around that time. At one of those events, the valedictorian of the class made this statement, "Most people fail because they give up what they want the most for what they want in the moment."

That one statement explains why so many Christians fail to make good decisions. They give up what they want most for what they want in the moment. They give up heaven for the momentary pleasures of life here and now. This was a mistake Moses refused to make. The book of Hebrews reminds us, "By faith Moses, when he became of age, refused to be called the son of Pharaoh's daughter, choosing rather to suffer affliction with the people of God than to enjoy the passing pleasures of sin, esteeming the reproach of Christ greater riches than the treasures in Egypt; for he looked to the reward" (Hebrews 11:24-26).

It is not easy give up the "now" for the "not yet" or the immediate for the eventual, but that is what Moses did. He refused to give up his eternal reward for the temporary pleasures and treasures of life on earth. If we follow his example, the Word of God promises that we will receive a rich welcome into eternal dwellings. One day, we will hear these words, "Well done, good and faithful servant ... enter into the joy of your lord" (Matthew 25:23).

Discussion Questions

1. How important is it to discuss the reality of heaven and hell?

2. Read 2 Corinthians 4:16-18 and then ask yourself why eternal decisions are difficult to make?

3. Name five ways hell is described in the Bible.

4. What are the most comforting descriptions of heaven in Revelation?

5. What decisions would we have to make to give up the "now" for the "not yet"?

Chapter 13

Learning From Our Mistakes

How to Handle Bad Decisions

Decisions are important. They affect your character, determine your destiny, and often come along with inescapable consequences. In order to consistently choose good over evil and God's best over what might be described as merely "good enough," we should strive to make Bible-based, God-glorifying, Christ-imitating, kingdom-seeking, Golden Rule-guided, prayer-saturated, influence-guarding, thought-purifying and eternity-minded decisions. But what if we try to do all of that and fail? What then? This question cannot be ignored. In fact, any discussion about making better decisions would be incomplete without making some effort to answer one final question, "How do you handle bad decisions?"

In his book, *The Carolina Way: Leadership Lessons From a Life in Coaching*, Hall of Fame basketball coach Dean Smith shared this helpful insight: "Our team's Thought for the Day concerning mistakes was 'Recognize it, admit it, learn from it, then forget it' " (Smith 282). I'd like to borrow Coach Smith's four-step plan for handling mistakes and apply it to our ongoing struggle to become more faithful Christians by making better decisions.

Recognize It

How do you handle bad decisions? The first thing you have to do is recognize it. When you fail to choose good over evil or right over wrong, you can't do anything to mend or improve your relationship with God until you recognize what you have done. But this first step is harder than it sounds. We all have a remarkable capacity to overlook sin in our lives. In fact, it is possible to see sin in other people and despise it without noticing that we are guilty of similar or, in some cases, much worse behavior. That is precisely what King David discovered when Nathan confronted him about the hidden sin in his life. Nathan told the king this familiar parable:

> There were two men in one city, one rich and the other poor. The rich man had exceedingly many flocks and herds. But the poor man had nothing, except one little ewe lamb which he had bought and nourished; and it grew up together with him and with his children. It ate of his own food and drank from his own cup and lay in his bosom; and it was like a daughter to him. And a traveler came to the rich man, who refused to take from his own flock and from his own herd to prepare one for the wayfaring man who had come to him; but he took the poor man's lamb and prepared it for the man who had come to him. (2 Samuel 12:1-4)

The Word of God tells us that when David heard that story his "anger was greatly aroused against the man, and he said to Nathan, 'As the LORD lives, the man who has done this shall surely die!'" (2 Samuel 12:5). Nathan promptly replied, "You are the man!" (v. 7). Is that not remarkable? David slept with another man's wife; he tried to deceive that man and when his deception failed he resorted to murder. Despite such egregious sins, David did not recognize that the villain in Nathan's story was not someone else; it was him. That story not only tells us something about David; it also says something about the rest of us. Much like the Pharisees, plenty of modern-day Christians can easily recognize the speck in someone else's eye even though they remain oblivious to the plank in their own (Matthew 7:3).

My wife's granddaddy used to tell the story about a man who came to church smelling like alcohol. He was in a battle with alcoholism, and in spite of his many relapses he continued reaching out to God for forgiveness and to his local church for help. Apparently, the people in that small congregation felt scandalized by his behavior. They criticized him sharply. Granddaddy, rather insightfully observed, "What if lust, greed or gossip had a distinct odor? What if others could smell our sins the way we smell alcohol?" Granddaddy was not trying to justify the sin of drunkenness; he was simply stating the obvious. It is easier to hide some sins than others, and for some strange reason we are much better at finding fault with other people than we are about recognizing sin in our own lives.

Why is this first step so important? It is important because, contrary to conventional wisdom, what you don't know can hurt you. For instance, what you don't know can hurt you physically. Plenty of people didn't know the harmful side effects of smoking. What they didn't know about smoking hurt them physically. They got sick and died from lung cancer. How many children have been severely burned because of what they didn't know about playing with fire? Just recently my 3-year-old nephew picked up his mother's curling iron. He did not know it was still plugged in and turned on. What he didn't know hurt him physically. He cried for three hours. He was in severe pain. What you don't know can hurt you physically, and it can hurt you spiritually as well. One of the most disturbing things Jesus ever said is recorded in Matthew 7:

> Not everyone who says to Me, "Lord, Lord," shall enter the kingdom of heaven, but he who does the will of My Father in heaven. Many will say to Me in that day, "Lord, Lord, have we not prophesied in Your name, cast out demons in Your name, and done many wonders in Your name?" And then I will declare to them, "I never knew you; depart from Me, you who practice lawlessness!" (Matthew 7:21-23)

What makes these words so unsettling? Jesus is describing people who thought they were ready to face God, but something was incomplete and out of place in the practice of their faith. They could see the good they had done and were able to tell Jesus, "We prophesied in Your name and cast out demons in Your name and did many wonders in Your name," but they were lost because in spite of the obvious good they had done they were also guilty of some form of lawlessness. Something was lacking in their service to God, and they didn't recognize it until it had become everlastingly too late.

Admit It

An event reportedly took place in the life of G.K. Chesterton. A *London Times* editorial asked the question, "What's wrong with the world today?" Chesterton supposedly responded with a simple but honest answer:

Sirs, what is wrong with the world today?
I am.
Sincerely,
G.K. Chesterton.

How do you handle bad decisions? You recognize them; but then much like Chesterton you have to admit them too. This second step can be just as difficult and uncomfortable as the first. We go to great lengths to cover up our sins. We deny sin in our lives. We minimize it, ignore it, justify it and rationalize it; but such behavior only makes bad decisions worse. The most important thing to do after you recognize sin in your life is to admit it – and the sooner the better. Thankfully, the Bible provides reliable models for us to follow:

• David: "Against You, You only, have I sinned, and done this evil in Your sight – that You may be found just when You speak, and blameless when You judge." (Psalm 51:4)

• Isaiah: "Woe is me, for I am undone! Because I am a man of unclean lips, and I dwell in the midst of a people of unclean lips; for my eyes have seen the King, the LORD of hosts." (Isaiah 6:5)

• Peter: "Depart from me, for I am a sinful man, O Lord!" (Luke 5:8)

• Paul: "This is a faithful saying and worthy of all acceptance, that Christ Jesus came into the world to save sinners, of whom I am chief." (1 Timothy 1:15)

• The Tax Collector: "God, be merciful to me a sinner!" (Luke 18:13)

• The Prodigal: "Father, I have sinned against heaven and before you, and I am no longer worthy to be called your son. Make me like one of your hired servants." (Luke 15:18-19)

Why is it so difficult for us to follow the example set by men like David, Isaiah, Peter and Paul? Fear is holding most of us back. We are afraid to share our spiritual failures with other people; after all, who wants to admit secret sins? Who wants to appear weak? Who wants to invite criticism? Nobody wants to do any of those things, but you can't get the help you need until you do.

Several years ago, a prominent couple in the congregation where I preach responded to the invitation and shared a very specific list of prayer requests. At the end of their written request, they made the following statement: "We believe in prayer, but the only way we can pray for each other and bear one another's burdens is to make them known."

If you are hurting and other Christians don't know it, they can't help. They can't pray for you because they don't even know the sins you have committed or the burdens you are carrying. However, if you share your spiritual struggles with fellow Christians, they can and will help. James taught first-century believers: "Confess your trespasses to one another, and pray for one another, that you may be healed. The effective, fervent prayer of a righteous man avails much" (James 5:16). If you are unwilling to admit mistakes to others, you have to do without the powerful assistance that comes from their prayers, and if you do not admit your sins to God you miss out on the forgiveness He has promised (1 John 1:9).

Learn From It

How do you handle bad decisions? Recognize them, admit them and learn from them. If we respond properly to bad decisions, they can actually bring about important changes and healthy growth in our lives. Coaches often claim their teams learn more from a painful loss than they do from an easy victory. Winning teams seldom feel the need to evaluate their weaknesses. The same thing could be said about every Christian. Sin has a way of stripping away the veneer. It reminds us of our brokenness and our constant need for God, and it gives us a clear picture of our spiritual condition: we are lost without Him.

After we recognize and admit sin, it is essential that we learn from it because God does not intend for us to "continue in sin" expecting "that grace may abound" (Romans 6:1). He wants us to learn from our mistakes so that we are not doomed to repeat them over and over again. The prodigal son is a good example of what it looks like to learn from your mistakes. The young man in Jesus' parable made plenty of mistakes. It was a mistake for him to ask for his inheritance; actually he didn't ask for it; he demanded it, and that was definitely a bad decision (Luke 15:12). It was a mistake to leave home, but he was too blinded by pride to know how big a mistake he was making at the time. It was a mistake to waste his inheritance on "prodigal living" (v. 13). He apparently never thought about what would happen to him when all his money was gone. That was a big mistake. Finally, it was a mistake for him to join himself to a citizen of that country; by so doing he only prolonged his suffering because that man didn't do anything to alleviate his misery (vv. 15-16).

The prodigal son made a lot of bad decisions, but he learned from his mistakes. He learned it was a lot better in his father's house than he thought it was before he left home (Luke 15:17). He learned, as we have been studying in this chapter, that it is better to admit mistakes than it is to ignore or deny them (v. 18). He learned when you need to make an important change in your life you should act on it immediately (v. 20). He learned when prodigals come home the father runs to welcome them (v. 20), and he also learned not everybody is happy when prodigals come home (v. 28), which leads us to our next point.

The older brother in this story also made some bad decisions. He decided not to forgive his rebellious younger brother (Luke 15:28). He decided harsh judgment is better than loving forgiveness (vv. 29-30). That mistake was more costly than he could have suspected. By judging his younger brother so mercilessly, he was setting the tone for his own eventual judgment (James 2:13). The older brother made another mistake that is all too common among religious people; he was guilty of self-righteousness; he actually believed he had never transgressed by breaking one of his father's commandments (Luke 15:29). He decided to wallow in envy, self-pity and ingratitude (vv. 29-30); his biggest mistake, however, was his failure to understand

and appreciate his father's grace (vv. 31-32). He decided not to go to the party (v. 28).

Everyone makes mistakes. In fact, Paul reminds us that "all have sinned and fall short of the glory of God" (Romans 3:23). It is all right to make a few mistakes as long as you learn from them. That's what the prodigal son did. He learned from his mistakes; but sadly, the older brother did not. Don't be like the older brother. When you make a bad decision and sin against God, recognize it, admit, learn from it and then forget about it and move on with your life. This final step may be the most challenging of all.

Forget It

Some of the people who are reading this book are haunted by the memory of past sins. Intellectually they know God has forgiven them, but they cannot let go of the past. Because they cannot forgive themselves, they relive their worst moments over and over again in their mind and go to sleep every night with a heavy heart and a guilty conscience. If the last few sentences sound all too familiar, then you need to understand this is not God's plan for you. God does not want you to spend the rest of your life in guilt, fear and regret. He wants you to move forward in hope, joy and gratitude.

That's why God gives us so many of the unflattering details of His greatest followers. When we read about great heroes in the Bible, it helps us to know that they were not perfect. Their stories give us confidence because if God could work in their imperfect lives, He can work in ours as well. Take for example, the pre-converted life of Paul.

He was "a blasphemer, a persecutor, and an insolent man" (1 Timothy 1:13). When Stephen was violently martyred, Paul (then Saul) was there "consenting to his death" (Acts 8:1). In the inspired words of Luke, Paul breathed out "threats and murder against the disciples of the Lord" (9:1); he persecuted followers of the way "to the death" and delivered "into prisons both men and women" (22:4), and he confessed before King Agrippa, "When they were put to death, I cast my vote against them" (26:10). Imagine the despair he must have felt when he heard these words from heaven, "I am Jesus, whom you are persecuting" (9:5). Paul was not just persecuting the church; he was persecuting Jesus. How do you come back from such a drastic mistake? Paul tells us in his own words in Philippians 3:

> Not that I have already attained, or am already perfected; but I press on, that I may lay hold of that for which Christ Jesus has also laid hold of me. Brethren, I do not count myself to have apprehended; but one thing I do, forgetting those things which are behind and reaching forward to those things which are ahead, I press toward the goal for the prize of the upward call of God in Christ Jesus. Therefore let us, as many as are mature, have this mind; and if in anything you think otherwise, God will reveal even this to you. (vv. 12-15)

Paul said, "Forgetting those things which are behind!" Here is the answer many of us have been seeking. The only way to move forward is to do what Paul did. After his baptism into Christ, he had to forget the past. He had to forget about the thoughts, words and deeds that were part of his life before Christ and without Christ. It was the only way he could move forward; it is also the one step still lacking for many of us who regret our bad decisions. We insist on remembering sins God has already forgiven because we still haven't forgiven ourselves. Maybe the best way for us to conclude is by returning to some of the wonderful promises God has made about forgiveness. When God forgives He:

- covers our sins (Psalm 85:2),
- casts all our sins behind His back (Isaiah 38:17),
- hides His face from our sins (Psalm 51:9),
- removes our transgressions from us as far as the east is from the west (Psalm 103:12),
- blots out our transgressions and sins (Isaiah 44:22),
- casts our sins into the depths of the sea (Micah 7:19),
- and remembers our sins and lawless deeds no more (Hebrews 8:12).

The cumulative and repetitive teaching of Scripture testifies to the fact that when God forgives He also forgets. Let that promise settle down into your anxious heart. If you have been washed by the blood of Jesus, you are fully forgiven. God has already forgotten your sins. Is it not time for you to do the same? We have all made some regrettable decisions, but once we have recognized them, admitted them and learned from them it is time to forget them. This is the only way we can press on and pursue better decisions in the future. Do not allow a sinful past to keep you from enjoying a glorious future with God. This might be the most important decision you ever make.

Discussion Questions

1. What did you do to fix things when you made bad decisions in life?

2. How did Nathan help David recognize his sin? What was David's response? What if David had responded differently?

3. Why are we afraid to admit our spiritual struggles with other Christians?

4. How can pride keep us from learning from our mistakes?

5. Why is it so hard for us as humans to forget the wrong things we do? Or the wrong things others do?

WORKS CITED

Beam, Joe. *Seeing the Unseen: A Handbook for Spiritual Warfare.* West Monroe: Howard, 1994.

Childress, Harvey A. *The Riches of Love.* Kearney: Morris, 2001.

Guinness, Os. *The Gravedigger File: Papers on the Subversion of the Modern Church.* Downers Grove: Intervarsity, 1983.

Howard, Alton H., comp. *Songs of the Church.* West Monroe: Howard, 1977.

King, Jason. "The Real McCoy." *Yahoo! Sports.* 16 Oct. 2008. 26 March 2015. <http://sports.yahoo.com/news/real/mccoy-021800812--ncaaf.html>.

MacArthur, John. *The MacArthur New Testament Commentary Philippians.* Chicago: Moody, 2001.

Maxwell, John C. *There's No Such Thing as "Business" Ethics: There's Only One Rule for Making Decisions.* New York: Center Street, 2003.

Ortberg, John. *Soul Keeping: Caring for the Most Important Part of You.* Nashville: Thomas Nelson, 2014.

Swindoll, Charles R. *Living Above the Level of Mediocrity: A Commitment to Excellence.* Waco: Word Books, 1987.

Smith, Dean. *The Carolina Way: Leadership Lessons From a Life in Coaching.* New York: Penguin, 2004.

ten Boom, Corrie. *The Hiding Place.* Uhrichsville: Barbour, 1971.